E. M. FORSTER

FRANCIS KING

E. M. FORSTER

with 122 illustrations

THAMES AND HUDSON

to KAY DICK

*First published in Great Britain 1978
First paperback edition 1988*

*Printed in Great Britain by
BAS Printers Limited,
Over Wallop, Hampshire*

The infant Forster clings to his mother, while she suffers his embrace. In later life, these positions came to be reversed.

EDWARD MORGAN FORSTER was born on 1 January 1879 at 6 Melcombe Place, Dorset Square, London NW1, the house of his parents. He died on 7 June 1970 in Coventry, at the home of his closest friend, Bob Buckingham, and Buckingham's wife, May. Next to these two events, the most important of his life was not, as for the majority of the human race, marriage but the death of his father from tuberculosis – a disease that had already carried off many of his brothers and sisters – in October 1880. That the boy should have become fatherless at the age of twenty-two months and that he should subsequently have been brought up exclusively by women, with no elder brother (a previous child had died at birth) and no other relatives in the house on whom to model himself, was the classic Freudian recipe for subsequent confusion about his sexual role.

Forster's beloved maternal grandmother, Louisa Whichelo, of whom he said: 'She was someone who knew how to live.'

Forster's mother, Alice Clara (Lily) Whichelo, lived on, an adored but also often resented matriarchal presence, to the age of ninety, dying in 1945. Her father had been a drawing-master who had earned a precarious living by teaching in a number of south London schools, among them Stockwell Grammar School. When he died suddenly and prematurely in 1867, he left his wife, Louisa, with ten children and no money to support them. Forster's maternal grandmother was obviously a remarkable woman – Mrs Honeychurch in *A Room with a View* was partly modelled on her – and, nothing daunted by her plight in those days before the Welfare State, she began to take in lodgers, usually Germans. As soon as her children reached an employable age,

often in their early teens, they were sent out into the world to earn their livings, the girls as governesses (the only female occupation then regarded as respectable) and the boys as clerks. The subsequent careers of the boys were often raffish and insecure.

Lily was luckier than most of her siblings. The family doctor, Mr Tayloe, was also doctor to Henry Thornton and his sister Marianne, by then alienated from each other for many years. The well-to-do, materialistic, pious, philistine Thorntons of Battersea Rise were leading members of the Clapham Sect – that 'industry in doing good' as William Cowper described it. Tayloe, kind, compassionate and eager to help the struggling widow, took Lily with him to East Side,

Henry Thornton's Oval Library at Battersea Rise, designed by William Pitt the Younger. It was the headquarters of most of the leaders of the anti-slavery movement.

the home of Marianne Thornton, then a formidable spinster of seventy, and of her 'resident niece', Henrietta Synnot. Mr Tayloe no doubt hoped that he would be able to persuade the two women to become patronesses to the delicate-featured, charming young girl, and he was not disappointed. They adopted her. But Marianne Thornton was not the kind of foster-mother that everyone would welcome. She insisted, when she took Lily for a holiday to Weymouth, that she should wear a shabby dress, despite Mr Tayloe's kind offers to finance a wardrobe to make her 'appear respectable', on the grounds that 'strays and waifs are never liked unless they show their lowly estate'. Subsequently, after Lily had been taught for some years by Henrietta, Marianne paid for her to attend a school kept by a Mademoiselle Collinet in Brighton, in order to prepare her for the inevitable career of governess. The jobs that followed were procured through Thornton influence – the last with a Mrs Farrer, *née* Wedgwood, who lived at Abinger, where Forster and his mother were subsequently to make their home for so many years.

One guesses that Marianne played the matchmaker between her protégée and her favourite nephew, Edward, son of her younger sister Laura and the Reverend Charles Forster. Forster himself took the view that his great-aunt had 'cared not for a "good" marriage but for a

Forster's father, Edward Morgan Llewellyn Forster

Drawing by Forster's father of St
Pierre, Coutances, 1873

marriage of true minds'; but one suspects that Edward Forster, for all
his talents, was something of an odd fish by the standards of the
Clapham Sect and that his aunt may have decided that an alliance
with a penniless, seemingly malleable girl, firmly under her own
control, might be the best thing for him. Edward had been educated at
Charterhouse and Trinity, Cambridge. When he came down, he
took up architecture under Arthur, later Sir Arthur, Blomfield –
another of whose pupils, a few years earlier, had been Thomas Hardy.
He had some promise as an architect, was witty in a sharp, feline way
and knew how to keep in favour with his aunt. But there was a
dreamy, unpractical side to his nature. This is exemplified by an event
at Forster's christening, at the age of two months, at Holy Trinity
Church on Clapham Common. The party walked over from

Marianne Thornton's house. Forster's father was evidently either in a state of perturbation or else abstracted, so that when, during the walk, the verger asked him what the baby was to be called, he gave his own names, Edward Morgan, instead of the names Henry Morgan under which the infant had already been registered. The verger wrote down 'Edward Morgan' on a piece of paper. The maternal grandmother, Louisa Whichelo, was holding the baby at the font, when the clergyman asked her what the baby was to be called. She could not find her voice and indicated the piece of paper in the verger's hand. Thus Forster became Edward instead of Henry.

When, not long after their marriage, the young couple went on a holiday to France, it is perhaps significant that a friend of the husband, called Streatfeild, should have accompanied them. It is perhaps equally significant that Marianne wrote to her protégée in Paris that she hoped that 'Eddie won't be too old maidish to walk you down the Boulevarde Italienne at night'. Eddie was then still in his twenties. Forster's attitude to the father whom he could not remember was always to be ambivalent. He kept safeguarded as 'treasured relics' the architectural sketches made in the course of travels in Italy and France – Eddie had, as Forster put it, 'a charming niggling pencil'; but though he provided Wilfred Stone with photographs of his mother for what is the best critical work about him, *The Cave and the Mountain*, he deliberately withheld any of his father. There seems no doubt that in some way Eddie was not an entirely satisfactory husband; and that Lily communicated to her son, whom she dominated throughout his life, a part of her dissatisfaction. Unlike his friend J. R. Ackerley, so remorseless in his determination to explore every inch of his father's 'secret orchard', Forster, who devoted a whole book to Marianne Thornton and, obliquely, to his whole Thornton ancestry, showed little desire to delve into his father's life or personality. When I once asked him 'What was your father like?', he answered with atypical tetchiness 'How should I know? He died before I was two.' In *Marianne Thornton* he declares that his father 'has always remained remote to me. I have never seen myself in him, and the letters from him and the photographs of him have not helped.' Yet, though Forster himself may not have seen himself in him, we may well do so.

Two and a half years after her husband's death, Lily and the infant Morgan moved to a house in Stevenage, Hertfordshire, called Rooksnest. This, the prototype of the much loved house in *Howards End*, was later to be the home of the composer Elizabeth Poston – whose family are supposed to have suggested the Wilcoxes to Forster. At that period, before the encroachment of urbanization, its setting was wholly rural. There was a sloping meadow similar to the one into which Helen Schlegel took her child to watch the haymaking; a similar wych elm ('leaning a little over the house, and standing on the

The tennis-court at Rooksnest, with
(*left to right*) Cousin Percy
(Whichelo), Aunt Rosie, Forster and
his mother

boundary between the garden and the meadow'); similar fir trees
blocking the view to the north. In part at least the young widow must
have decided to move into the country out of a fear that, in the polluted
air of London, her son might contract the disease that had killed his
father. (She was to transmit to Forster this excessive concern for his
health until, in his middle years, he suddenly realized how robust he
really was.) But one also surmises that a woman who was later herself
to become so dominant may have resented, as she grew older and more
self-confident, the continuing domination of the ageing Marianne
(aptly called 'Aunt Monie'). There was the added complication that
the 'resident niece', Henrietta Synnot, no doubt jealous of the younger
and more attractive woman, had changed from being an affectionate
protectress – only four years previously she had been present as
godmother at the infant Morgan's christening – to an implacable
enemy. By 1887, even when under the same roof at East Side, the two
women were only communicating with each other by letters or verbal
messages delivered by the maids. But none the less mother and son paid
frequent visits to Clapham from the country. Morgan had by then
succeeded his father as favourite nephew and had acquired what he

himself called 'the deplorable nickname' of 'the Important One'. Any fatherless, only child so called might be expected to become priggish and self-satisfied; and there is evidence to suggest that Forster was no exception. (The hostile might even suggest that the priggishness and self-satisfaction remained with him.) It was at East Side that Forster discovered, at the precocious age of four, that he was able to read to himself. When his aunt's nurse summoned him from his upstairs room to join the grown-ups below, he admonished her with the words 'Tiresome to be interrupted in my reading when the light is so good. Can't you tell the people I am busy reading?' No, not an entirely attractive child. It was at East Side too that one of his cousins reduced him to prolonged screaming by blowing a whistle in his ear. Like many another over-protective mother, Lily was angry both with the bully for teasing her loved one and with 'Poppy' (one of her pet-names for him) for not being able to stick up for himself.

Apart from teaching himself to read at the age of four, Forster gave other indications of precocity. A new maid, Emma, arrived at Rooksnest, and the little boy decided to pass on to her the dancing-lessons that he was receiving from his mother. Clutching her to him, he would whirl her around the room in a clumsy attempt at the polka. When Emma called Jupiter a star, he was quick to put her right; when she confused astronomy and botany, he showed his scorn. Finally Emma was dismissed. She and the child had quarrelled over a basket of primroses that they had managed to upset between them. 'But I had to hit Master Morgan, ma'am, he hit me.' Lily did not accept the excuse. No, not an entirely attractive child.

In the Forster household, as in most upper-middle-class households of that period, morning prayers were a daily routine. But, at a time when republicanism was far more fashionable in England than it is now, this respect for God did not preclude a lack of respect for the monarchy. In 1887 Queen Victoria was celebrating her Jubilee and loyal citizens were contributing their pennies towards a present for her. Lily was anti-Jubilee and her son, not unnaturally, followed suit. But when he actually saw the old queen driving in her carriage to nearby Hatfield House and felt the stern eyes of a policeman upon him, he joined everyone else in waving and cheering. In similar fashion, throughout his future life, he was to combine the holding of unorthodox opinions with a respect for the law.

It was during this decade at Stevenage that Forster made friends with a succession of garden boys, the chief of whom was Ansell. The importance of the relationship with Ansell is indicated by the two facts that this 'snub-nosed pallid even-tempered youth' gave his name to a key character in *The Longest Journey* and that he was also obviously the inspiration of the posthumously published short story 'Ansell' in *The Life to Come*. Written in about 1902, this story tells of how a

Aunt Monie insisted that the infant Forster should look as much like Little Lord Fauntleroy as possible. Drawing by George Richmond

Cambridge scholar – as it were, Forster himself – gives up his dissertation on the Greek optative for life with a former garden boy, now gamekeeper, with whom he roams the countryside, heedless of the future. The real-life Ansell used to be let off work every Wednesday afternoon in order to play with the son of his mistress. There was a great deal of horse-play; but, unlike the hero of the short story, who is content to lapse into a mindless hedonism, the young Forster did not neglect his friend's education, reading to him from *The Swiss Family Robinson* and attempting to inculcate the rudiments of arithmetic – with little success.

It is clear that this period of less than ten years from the age of four to almost fourteen was always to represent for Forster a kind of Earthly Paradise. Though the house was only rented, not inherited or bought, it was there that he felt that his roots had gone down deep. Through the years ahead he was to be a regular visitor. Even as an old man, in

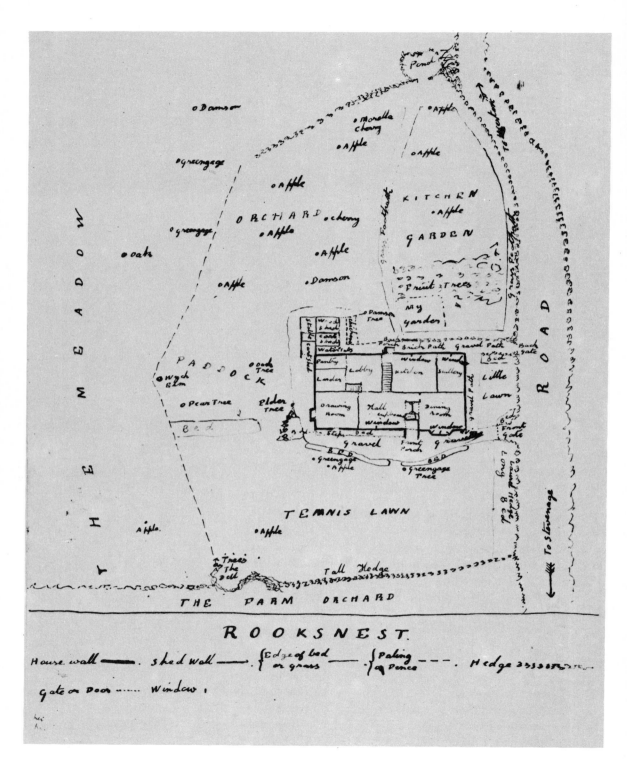

ROOKSNEST.

House wall ▬▬▬ Shed Wall ▬▬ Edge of bed or grass ▬▬ Paling or fence ▬ ▬ ▬ Hedge ꙮꙮꙮꙮ

Gate or Door ⋯⋯ Window ∎

1941, he called there and looked in at the neighbouring farm to see whether another of his childhood playmates, Frankie Franklyn, was still alive (Forster was to know five generations of his family); and when, in 1960, he heard that the house was threatened with being pulled down, he was deeply upset.

The arrival of 'a snobbish Irish tutor' both obliterated Ansell – who 'probably did more than anyone towards armouring me against life' – and was the first ominous hint that this world of prelapsarian happiness and innocence was about to vanish forever. At the age of eleven he was dispatched to a preparatory school, Kent House, in Eastbourne kept by a Mr C.P. Hutchinson. The boys bullied him there and the staff regarded him as a spoiled mother's darling. He was deeply unhappy. While out walking by himself, he suffered one of those traumatic incidents in which, in later years, it is difficult even for the victim to distinguish between truth and fantasy. Forster would

The drawing room at Rooksnest during the Forsters' occupancy. Many of the objects remained around Forster all his life.

Opposite: Forster's own map of Rooksnest – of which he wrote: 'The house is my childhood and safety.'

Kent House, Eastbourne. Forster –
nicknamed 'Mousie' by his
schoolfellows – is in the middle of
the front row.

revert to it in conversation, even in old age, as though still trying to puzzle it out. A man had exposed himself to him; the child, half horrified and half thrilled, may even have masturbated him. Later, guilty and excited, he had reported the matter to the headmaster and had enjoyed the subsequent fuss. The man was never apprehended. Lily had rushed down to the school to find out for herself exactly what had happened.

At the age of fourteen Forster said goodbye to Rooksnest, after he and his mother had been ousted by the owners. It was a banishment paralleled by, and even more devastating than, his banishment, more than a half century later, from West Hackhurst, the house in which he and his mother had lived together for so many years until her death. In the course of a paper on 'Memory' read to the Bloomsbury Memoir Club in the 1930s, he referred to the event and then went on to say: 'If I had been allowed to stop on there, I should have become a different person, married, and fought in the war.' The claim is an odd one. He might well have grown up physically more impressive if he had continued to live a life of country pursuits. But, whether resident at Stevenage or elsewhere, he would always have been a part of an exclusively female household of mother and two maids, and it is hard to see how his essential nature would have been changed in any way.

At about the same time as the departure from the beloved house, he entered Tonbridge School and so embarked on a period of his life even more unhappy than that at preparatory school. In his entry in *Who's Who*, Forster would put, under Education, 'Tonbridge School (dayboy)'. A significant parenthesis. Like the governesses that so many of his maternal aunts had become and that his mother had been until her marriage, dayboys at this minor public school, as at public schools more distinguished, suffered the worst of both worlds. The governesses belonged neither among the family nor among the servants but somewhere in between. The dayboys were a shallow step above state school boys and a steep step below the privileged boarders. Forster for all his life had a deep-seated loathing of the public-school system and this is nowhere expressed more strongly than in *The Longest Journey*, in which middle-class, middle-brow, conventional Tonbridge is represented as 'Sawston' (the name itself grates), where the hero Rickie goes to be a master. In a mock end-of-term speech that he composed for *The Spectator* in 1933, Forster's bitterness was still strong: 'School was the unhappiest time of my life. . . . From this platform of middle age, this throne of experience, this altar of wisdom, this scaffold of character, this beacon of hope, this threshold of decay, my last words to you are: "There's a better time coming."' How different from Cyril Connolly, for whom no subsequent happiness could measure up to that of his years at Eton. For Forster the English public school was always to

Forster, aged eleven

'Forster? The writer? Yes, I remember him. A little cissy. We took it out of him, I can tell you.' (one of his schoolmates, in later years)

Forster with his mother – at a time when, unknown to him, she had decisively rejected more than one proposal of marriage

represent the things that he most hated in English life: philistinism; snobbery; the bland assumption of racial and class superiority; above all (an obsession of his) the 'undeveloped heart'. Yet it seems likely that, in retrospect, Forster exaggerated the horror of his schooldays. As a dayboy, though he may certainly have been teased and even bullied because of his comparatively lowly status, he had the comforts of his home and the protective presence of his mother to which to retreat at the end of every day; and the headmaster was at least sufficiently tolerant to allow this muff of a boy to bicycle around the countryside instead of playing the games obligatory for everyone else.

The Longest Journey carries a hint that, although Forster welcomed his mother's extreme protectiveness, he also – with an ambivalence that was to remain with him for the rest of her life – resented it. This comes in Rickie's guilty recollection of an occasion when his now dead mother – 'a woman beautiful without and within' – nags at him

about wearing a greatcoat against the cold (Forster himself would often wear a muffler in the most unseasonable weather) until, exasperated beyond endurance, he rushes out of the house, slamming the door.

Rickie passes from public school, where he has been 'cold and friendless and ignorant', to Cambridge, which 'had taken and soothed him, and warmed him, and had laughed at him a little, saying that he must not be so tragic yet awhile'. Forster himself experienced a similar revelation and renewal when, at the age of seventeen, he left Tonbridge and made his way to King's College, Cambridge.

Body and spirit, reason and emotion, work and play, architecture and scenery, laughter and seriousness, life and art – these pairs which are elsewhere contrasted were there fused into one. People and books reinforced one another, intelligence joined hands with affection, speculation became a passion, and discussion was made profound by love.

Rooksnest: Forster and his mother at rear; Charlie Poston (neighbour) and Alice Alford seated on hammock; Aunt Rosie (who married Robert Alford) in front

Forster is describing the advent of Goldsworthy Lowes Dickinson at Cambridge; but it might be of his own advent that he is writing.

Forster occupied a set of rooms, W7, on the top floor of Bodley's neo-Gothic building, with splendid views of Queens' garden from the bedroom and of King's and Clare bridges from the sitting-room. There is a board that records all the names of the inhabitants over the years and Forster's is among them. It has usually been assumed that it was in this set of rooms that, in *The Longest Journey*, Rickie and his friends held their celebrated discussion about the nature of reality – is a cow in a field when there is no one there to see it? Forster began by reading Classics, taking a Second in the Tripos, and then – having been awarded an Exhibition by the college – switched to History, with a Second again. His study of the Classics enabled him, six years after he had gone down from Cambridge, to contribute an introduction and notes to a translation of the *Aeneid* by E. Fairfax Taylor.

Forster at about the time when he became one of the 'Apostles'

Opposite: The cover (12 November 1900) of a King's College magazine, to which Forster contributed a whimsical little skit on Aeschylus's *Agamemnon*, entitled 'A Tragic Interior'

BASILEONA

Contents.

No. 2

More importantly, it brought him into contact, as tutor, with Nathaniel Wedd, a brash, formidably intelligent, iconoclastic figure, who 'wore a red tie, blasphemed, and taught Dickinson [Goldsworthy Lowes Dickinson] how to swear too – always a desirable accomplishment for a high-minded young don . . .'. As an undergraduate, Wedd had been conscious that, not having been educated at Eton but at the City of London School, he could never become one of the 'Best Set'. He therefore set about outraging it by such exploits as inviting Bernard Shaw, then regarded as the John the Baptist of Red Revolution, to come and address one of the college societies. One can imagine the effect of someone as robust as Wedd on someone as timorous as the youthful Forster. Although he subsequently married, Wedd was one of those teachers to whom a latent homophilia gives a rare degree of understanding of, and sympathy with, the problems of the young. Even as an old man, he still exerted a strong influence and attraction. Patrick Wilkinson, himself

an eminent Classical scholar at the same college, recollects how he 'envied him the immediate contact he established with pupils, so that what had begun as Latin prose supervision might end with the pupil confiding to this septuagenarian the intimacies of his life, his family, his love affairs, his hopes and fears'. Of Wedd, Forster himself wrote: 'It is to him . . . more than to anyone that I owe such awakening as has befallen me.' This awakening included a loss of faith in Christianity. Wedd was an atheist. He is usually identified as the don (though the remark has also been ascribed to A. E. Housman) who commented about some unusually tough meat in Hall: 'This lamb is even more hard to swallow than the Lamb of God.' Reproved for playing croquet on the sabbath, he is said to have retorted: 'What is the use of believing in a faith so fragile that it can't survive the click of croquet balls?' This kind of abrasive wit, so like that of Samuel Butler, another potent but later influence on Forster, must have been far more persuasive than any rhetoric or earnest argument.

It was Wedd who first introduced Forster to such 'revolutionary' writers of the day as Ibsen; and when Forster began to contribute to university magazines essays with such titles as 'On Bicycling' or 'On Grinds', it was an Ibsen hero, Peer Gynt, whose name he took at first for his pseudonym. Since it is difficult to see even the most tenuous connection between Ibsen's character, so greedy for experience of the world that lies before him, and Forster, who shrank from it in fastidious timidity, the choice is inexplicable. The tone of these early contributions is blandly anodyne; one might be reading a copy of *Punch* of the period.

It is not surprising that Forster was more influenced by his 'cynical, aggressive, Mephistophelian' Classics tutor than by his History tutor, Oscar Browning. No two men could have been less alike than Wedd and Browning. Browning had returned to King's, of which he was already a Fellow, after a period (1860–75) as a master at Eton. His years at Eton had been glorious ones, with his beautiful mother acting as hostess both to the aristocratic and eminent and to the boys whom he invited, with an impartial lavishness of hospitality, to his house. At his entertainments only one subject was tabu to the boys: athletics. Unfortunately a homosexual scandal suddenly obliged him to leave the college; but, with the extraordinary resilience that always characterized his career, he had soon adjusted himself to a diminution of income from £3,000 to £300 per annum (the worth of his Fellowship) and had once again established himself as one of the most vivid and controversial of Cambridge figures. 'I came towards the end of O.B.'s glory,' Forster wrote, 'nor was I ever part of his train. But he shines out with a magnificence which has been withheld from his admirable detractors, he remains as something unique in the history of the university, a deposit of radium, a mass of equivocal fire.'

Oscar Browning, caricatured in *Vanity Fair*, 1888

Opposite, above: Roger Fry portrait of Goldsworthy Lowes Dickinson, 1893

Opposite, below: Nathaniel Wedd, with wife

23

King's College group: Forster *top left*; H.O. Meredith *fourth from right, second row*

Browning did not care that at Cambridge, as at Eton, his extravagances would often arouse moralistic disapprobation. He tended to choose his male secretaries for their youth and their looks rather than for their proficiency. Like Maurice Bowra, who would disport himself in the nude at Parson's Pleasure at Oxford at a later date, Browning would constantly be found exposing his corpulence at the Cambridge swimming club. Forster would have preferred to go to Goldsworthy Lowes Dickinson than to Oscar Browning for tutorials; but he was, as he put it, 'dished' by Browning, who insisted that he must go to him. In consequence it was 'to the handkerchief which covered O.B.'s face' that Forster read out his fortnightly essays on Wallenstein or Louis XIV.

Eventually, Browning was obliged to leave Cambridge, as he had been obliged to leave Eton. He settled in Rome, complaining about 'plots' against him, and inevitably had soon made himself into a prominent member of the large Anglo-American community. While there, in the equivocal words of his entry in the *Dictionary of National Biography* (written by Dickinson), 'he assisted young Italians, as he had done young Englishmen, towards the openings they desired.'

Browning was a snob; he was flamboyant; he was boastful; he was often insincere. Forster in turn was mousy, dowdy, plain, quiet and middle class. There was no basis for friendship between the two men other than a community of sexual interest – which, at that period, Forster would never have betrayed.

Although, later in life, he was to become Goldsworthy Lowes Dickinson's disciple, his biographer and one of his closest friends, Forster did not get to know him well until he had gone down from Cambridge. They met chiefly through Lowes Dickinson's Discussion Society, which differed from other college societies in that Dickinson himself presided, as at a seminar. Members drew lots to speak and the one rule was that no one should ever say anything that he did not believe to be true. Dickinson obviously had no use for the kind of playful sophistry that undergraduates so often practise in order to exercise their wits.

Another and better known society was the Apostles, which Forster joined, in his last year at Cambridge, through a fellow undergraduate and close friend, H. O. ('Hom') Meredith. The Apostles had come into existence in the 1820s, originally with the title 'The Cambridge Conversazione Society'. When Forster arrived on the scene, it was about to enter on its period of greatest glory, with such people as the philosophers McTaggart, Bertrand Russell and Alfred North Whitehead and the writers Lytton Strachey, Desmond MacCarthy and Leonard Woolf among its members.

Forster was to write admiringly of the Apostles and other similar Cambridge societies:

No one who has once felt their power will ever become a good mixer or a yes-man. Their influence, when it goes wrong, leads to self-consciousness and superciliousness; when it goes right, the mind is sharpened, the judgement is strengthened, and the heart becomes less selfish.

Many subsequent members of the Bloomsbury Group – John Maynard Keynes, Roger Fry, Desmond MacCarthy, Leonard Woolf and Thoby Stephen (Virginia Woolf's brother, who was to die at the tragically early age of twenty-six in 1906) – were members of the Apostolic Ring at the same time as Forster. Although, in his Life of John Maynard Keynes, Roy Harrod describes Virginia Woolf and Vanessa Bell as 'Apostles to the finger-tips', women were not, of course, then admitted to the Society. Virginia Woolf resented this exclusion, writing petulantly to Lytton Strachey in 1912: 'It's all Cambridge – that detestable place; and the ap-s-les are so unreal, and their loves are so unreal, and yet I suppose it's all going on still swarming in the sun – and perhaps not as bad as I imagine. But when I think of it, I vomit – that's all – a green vomit. . . .' When, more than half a century after Forster was admitted as an Apostle, it was proposed that membership should be thrown open to women, it is interesting that he should have disapproved of the idea.

It was during this period that Lytton Strachey gave Forster the nickname of 'the Taupe' – 'partly', as Leonard Woolf put it,

'because of his faint physical resemblance to a mole, but principally because he seemed intellectually and emotionally to travel unseen underground and every now and again pop up unexpectedly with some subtle observation or delicate quip which somehow or other he had found in the depths of the earth or of his own soul'.

Forster's epiphany at Cambridge has tended to be presented as an intellectual one; but like Rickie's in *The Longest Journey*, it was more in the nature of a spiritual emergence into sunlight after a long trudge through a dark and dank tunnel. Since he was intuitively penetrative rather than intellectually powerful in the manner of his fellow Apostles Russell, Keynes and G. E. Moore, what impressed him in the Apostolic Ring was not so much what was said but the freedom that made it possible to be said at all. All the things that had previously aroused his private opposition – the smug materialism of his Thornton ancestors, the orthodoxies of public service, patriotism and good form inculcated at Tonbridge – were now being openly attacked by spirits kindred to him. The influence of Moore's *Principia ethica* has tended to be exaggerated. Forster himself declared that he 'could not remember having read' the book that Keynes welcomed as 'the opening of a new heaven on a new earth'; and anyone who had read it, would be unlikely to forget that he had done so. If Moore influenced him, it was through the medium of others.

What Forster also derived from the Apostles, as later from the Bloomsbury Group, was the sense of belonging to an élite, a Blessed Band of Brothers, who could afford to despise and patronize the 'Stumpfs' (their slang for the Philistines) and those who were not 'saved' (a term used by Rickie in *The Longest Journey*). Such an apparent exclusiveness would have a potent appeal for a young man previously isolated by his status as a fatherless only child, as a despised dayboy and as an unacknowledged homosexual. There was also the gratification, both within the little ring of the Apostles and within the slightly larger ring of Cambridge, of finding himself in an almost exclusively masculine environment after so many years of living in an almost exclusively feminine one. Further, this almost exclusively masculine environment was also a largely homophile – though not homosexual – one at King's at this period. This does not mean, of course, that there was any open discussion of the topic, such as is now commonplace at English universities, with their Gay Socs and Gay Groups and their invitations to well-known homosexuals to come and address them. 'Sex was not mentioned in Cambridge in those days,' Forster himself has written, 'that is to say, not in the small circle I knew.' There is no reason to disbelieve him. When George Barger – later Professor of Chemistry at Edinburgh – gave a talk on Sex to Dickinson's Discussion Society, Dickinson took the precaution of ensuring that only 'serious-minded youths' attended.

From within the protection of the Apostolic Ring, Forster, like Dickinson, could either totally ignore or else look down on what he called 'the other two Cambridges'. One of these was 'the Cambridge of the organising and the researching don. Stuffy yet raw, parochial yet colourless. . . .' The other was the Cambridge of the undergraduate who 'takes pass-degrees, roars around the football fields, sits down in the middle of Hammersmith Broadway after the boat race . . .'. Thus were the inhabitants of darkness dismissed by the radiant elect, the 'Stumpfs' by the Saved.

Throughout Forster's work and thought the simple antithesis of Cambridge/Sawston, of inner circle of illumination and outer darkness, is always present. But the antithesis is merely a repetition of an older one between the scatty, impoverished, improvident, Bohemian, good-hearted Whichelos and the disciplined, wealthy, righteous, conventional, unspontaneous Thorntons. There is also another antithesis, ever-recurrent and yet never presented except in disguise and with a strange ambivalence of feeling, and that is between the cosy, protective, dainty, civilized, feminine world of his mother and the tough, harsh, uneducated, dangerous world of the kind of men who increasingly attracted him as he grew older.

When Forster left Cambridge, he was under no immediate obligation to seek a job. This was because his great-aunt Marianne Thornton had left him a sum of £8,000 on her death. With typical Thornton providence, she had stipulated that he was not to receive the capital until he was twenty-five; and that in the meantime the interest

Aunt Laura at West Hackhurst. She was always active in furthering Forster's career and eventually left him the lease of the house.

was to be used for his education. It was this money that took him to Tonbridge; it was also this money that, more happily, took him to Cambridge. It then enabled him to travel about Europe, notably to Italy and Greece. Forster concludes his Life of Marianne Thornton with a reference to this legacy: 'She and no one else made my career as a writer possible, and her love, in a most tangible sense, followed me beyond the grave.' Yet, ironically, it may be that, by cushioning her nephew with a small private income, Marianne Thornton prevented him from becoming a great novelist, rather than an extremely good one. If he had been obliged to plunge out into the sea of life amid a press of other swimmers, he might finally have achieved more than by sitting, detached and increasingly indolent, in the deckchair she had rented for him on the shore. Unfortunately few writers are in a position to choose the exact amount of *Sturm und Drang* necessary for them to fulfil their potential. Gissing is an example of a writer who could have done with less; Forster of one who could have done with more. If Forster had been more familiar with the processes by which decisions are reached, money is made and people are coerced or persuaded into working with each other, the Wilcoxes in *Howards End* and those Burtons and Turtons whom he so much derided in *A Passage to India* might have been characters born out of knowledge rather than caricatures created out of prejudice.

Before setting out from England, Forster did, however, toy with the idea of a career for himself. In similar circumstances, Rickie of *The Longest Journey* opted to become a schoolmaster and it was along these lines that Forster made a number of tentative approaches, notably to Oscar Browning. But Browning, who usually showed better judgement about people than about events, was 'amiable but not encouraging'. Forster's two Seconds needed, in Browning's view, some fortifying and he suggested a certificate from a training college – possibly from the one over which he himself presided in Cambridge, in addition to all his other duties and avocations. But Forster drifted away from the idea and probably it was just as well. As a schoolmaster, it is unlikely that he would have been any more of a success than Rickie or any more happy. Though in later years he learned to impose his will, quietly but with total effectiveness, he was then too unauthoritative in character and too frail in physique to perform a task usually essential to the successful handling of schoolboys.

So it was that he decided on an extended period of travel in Europe. Most young men in similar circumstances would have set off either alone or in the company of someone – male at that period, for reasons of propriety – of approximately their own age. But the *pensioni* of Rome, Tuscany and the Riviera were full of widows eking out modest incomes from inherited capital (the capital itself must never, of course, be touched) in the company of their spinster daughters; and it was a

What would have been seen from the Room with a View. The Lungarno, Florence, near where the Forsters stayed in 1901

simulacrum of this situation that was now created, as Mother came too – after the rather dreary, semi-detached house at 10 Earl's Road, Tunbridge Wells, had been given up and the furniture placed in storage.

The story of the journey south in those days before aeroplanes and package tours was the familiar one of arguments with avaricious porters, sudden panics that the luggage had been mislaid or stolen, and stomachs upset by food too rich and unfamiliar. The Forsters stopped for ten days at Cadenabbia, the setting on Lake Como of that remarkable literary sport *Madame Solario* by 'Madame Solario' (Gladys Huntingdon) – a novel published after the Second World War that might, in every particular, be describing the little resort as it was when the Forsters visited it. From there they moved to Milan and then to Florence, to the Pensione Simi. This, like the Jennings-Riccioli – another claimant to the distinction of being the place in which Lucy and Charlotte in *A Room with a View* took up residence – was presided over by a Cockney *patronne*. Through an introduction from his musicologist friend, E. J. Dent – best known now to the general public for his translations of Mozart's operas – Forster met R. H. Cust, a dilettante art-historian, author of *The Pavement Artists of Siena*, who was one of a group of homosexual expatriates then resident in the city. But for the most part, here and elsewhere in Italy, the people with whom the Forsters mixed were neither such foreign residents nor Italians, but fellow tourists like themselves, most of them female and most of them obliged to be careful about their pennies. From time to time Lily had cause to complain about her son, who tended to lose things and forget things and was, as through all his life, 'hopelessly impractical'.

Cortona, Assisi and Perugia followed. Apart from her complaints and worries about 'poor Morgan', Lily often found her fellow tourists irritating. The English offended her on a number of occasions by being 'common'. One of them, a great-aunt of Stephen Spender, smoked and told 'amusing' stories – by which Lily was obviously not amused. The Americans, over-friendly and loud-voiced, were just as bad.

In Rome, Forster had two accidents in quick succession, first falling down the stairs of the *pensione* and spraining his ankle and then falling up the steps of St Peter's and fracturing an arm. These disasters put him even more at the mercy of a host of middle-aged women, led by his mother, who was obliged to wash him like a baby and commented how much cleaner he looked as a consequence. He was doing some desultory writing, switching to his left hand now that his right was out of commission; but, as he records in his introduction to the *Collected Short Stories* (1947), it was not until, in the following spring, the Forsters went south, to Naples, to Sicily and then back to Naples, that his imagination was stirred to produce something other than notebook jottings, travel essays and the abortive beginning of a novel. The result was his 'The Story of a Panic', the first chapter of which 'rushed into my mind' in the Vallone Fontana Caroso, a few miles north of Ravello, where he had been wandering on his own. It is rarely possible to pinpoint the exact moment when an author discovers his essential identity; but in Forster's case it would seem to have been then. Some critics have seen this fantasy about the appearance of the Great God Pan to a fourteen-year-old schoolboy as an allegory of Forster's own sexual awakening. The boy is on holiday with two aunts, who stifle him with their protectiveness. 'Naturally enough,' writes the narrator, 'his features were pale, his chest contracted, and his muscles undeveloped. His aunts thought him delicate; what he really needed was discipline.' The description might be one of Forster himself at the same age. Once the God possesses him, the boy is wholly changed. His response to the solicitude of the rest of the party alternates between silence and over-excited gabbling; with an intimacy that shocks his fellow tourists he embraces a fisherman turned waiter at the *pensione*; and at night, refusing to be confined to the womb of his room, he leaps from the window and races about the countryside. Pan, representing an elemental sexuality, also appears in 'The Curate's Friend',

The Wood Boy by Arthur H. Buckland. *Fin-de-siècle* English literature was full of Pan, as the apotheosis of nature and 'naturalness', in opposition to urbanization and over-civilization.

prompting the reader to agree with Forster in his judgement in *Howards End*: 'Of Pan and the elemental forces the public has heard a little too much – they seem Victorian.'

The Forsters continued to linger in Italy, despite some brisk advice from G. M. Trevelyan, the historian, in a letter. 'You ought to get *study or employment*, to get your teeth into, other than the shallower side of intricate psychology.' He goes on to admonish Forster with considerable insight: 'One has to make oneself first; the work will then find itself out and follow.' His 'jaw' (as he himself terms it) concludes: 'England, with all its faults . . . is a better place than invalids and tennis players in Italian hotels', followed by the suggestion that Forster might take up teaching at the Working Men's College. One of the places that followed in the itinerary was San Gimignano – 'Monteriano' of *Where Angels Fear to Tread*. Shortly after the last war, an ancient native of the town, supporting himself on a stick, would take tourists up and down the towers and, with many a nudge and wink, imply that he and Forster had been lovers. At that period of Forster's life and with Lily along, it seems most unlikely.

Forster (*second from right*) in a street in
Rhodes, during his Greek travels,
1903

Eventually the two travellers arrived back in England. They took
up temporary residence in the Kingsley Hotel in Bloomsbury (it is still
in existence), so as to be near the Working Men's College in Great
Ormond Street, where Forster had been engaged to take a weekly class
in Latin – not a particularly arduous duty. Also teaching a weekly
class there was his close friend from Cambridge, H. O. Meredith, a
better Classical scholar. Forster once described Meredith to J. R.
Ackerley as 'my first great love'; but, though the importance of the
relationship to Forster is not in doubt, its exact nature must remain
obscure. Meredith, a basically heterosexual man, probably took the
physical lead, either out of kindness or out of curiosity, but Forster was
the one who was in love. Meredith's subsequent life seems not to have
been changed by whatever took place between them; but Forster's was
changed radically and forever. As so often in relationships in which
one has been the lover and the other the acquiescing loved one, there is
usually an aftermath of resentment on the part of the former lover.
Thus it was that Forster grew increasingly impatient and dismissive of
the man whom he had once seen as holding the golden key to the
prison of his pent-up sexuality.

Apart from his one class at the College, Forster had no success in finding employment and so, in the spring, he decided to go on a Greek cruise. On this occasion, Lily was dumped in Florence, once again at the Pensione Simi, with a female friend, and Forster then joined the ship alone. It was an extremely academic affair, devoted more to scholarship than to pleasure. Wedd was another of the travellers; the tour-conductor was the distinguished archaeologist E. A. Gardner. Near Olympia Forster suffered an epiphany similar to that in the isolated valley above Ravello and 'The Road from Colonus', one of the most subtle of his short stories, came into being.

He returned to Florence to pick up his mother and there he, she and E. J. Dent went to the opera to hear the great soprano Tetrazzini, then at the outset of her prodigious career, sing in *Lucia di Lammermoor*. He was later to use the experience to great effect in *Where Angels Fear to Tread*.

Luisa Tetrazzini at a time, after Forster had heard her in 1903, when her fame had spread to every corner of the world

E.J. Dent, in Bologna, 1903. He was to achieve fame as a musicologist and translator of libretti, especially those for Mozart's operas.

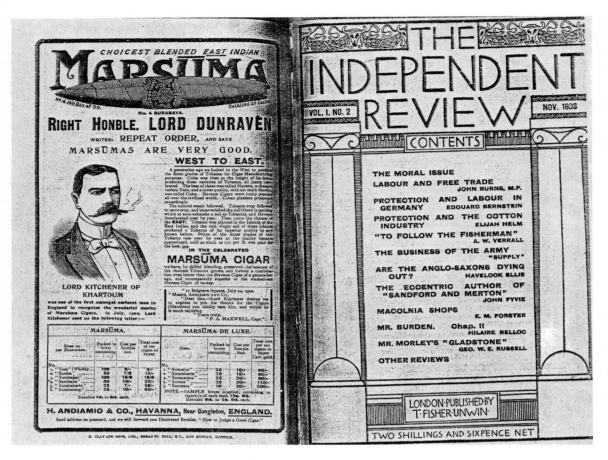

Front and back covers of the *Independent Review*. Front cover designed by Roger Fry

On his return to England with his mother, Forster began to contribute to the *Independent Review*, the first number of which appeared in 1903. Edward Jenks, a lawyer now forgotten, was the editor. The editorial board consisted, among others, of such Forster friends as Goldsworthy Lowes Dickinson, G. M. Trevelyan and Wedd. Roger Fry, another friend, designed the cover. The review was a political, not a literary, one, its chief policy being to combat the aggressive imperialism and protectionism of Joseph Chamberlain. While later admitting that the *Independent Review* 'did not make much difference to the councils of the nation', Forster none the less claimed for it that 'Those who were Liberals felt that the heavy, stocky body of their party was about to grow wings and leave the ground. Those who were not Liberals were equally filled with hope: they saw avenues opening into literature, philosophy, human relationships.' To his generation it appeared 'as a light rather than a fire, but a light that penetrated the emotions'. His first contribution was an essay 'Macolnia Shops' – a charming account, later included in *Abinger Harvest*, of how

a Roman matron buys a Greek toilet-case as a present for her daughter and of how, centuries later, it lands up in the Kirchner Museum in Rome. It was followed by other essays and some of his early short stories.

In the spring of 1904 the Forsters settled in a flat, 11 Drayton Court in Drayton Gardens, London SW10. This was their first experience of flat life and they did not take to it. The rooms were small and few, the outlook was hemmed in, the street was noisy. But it was convenient, since, in addition to his weekly class at the Working Men's College, Forster had now also begun to lecture on Italian art and history for the Cambridge Local Lectures Board. These were lonely years, when he knew that he was doomed (as he saw it) to be a homosexual and feared that he would never find the Ideal Friend for whom he so much craved. But this very loneliness intensified his literary activity, just as sexual fulfilment was later to slow it down, and short stories poured out of him with a fecundity astonishing when one thinks of the long period of aridity at the end of his life. For criticism

When F.D. Maurice founded the Working Men's College in 1854, he declared: 'We came forward to help the working man that we might help ourselves.'

'Turn where he would, it encircled him . . . this double entrenchment of the Rings.' 'Cadbury Rings' in *The Longest Journey* were suggested by Figsbury Ring.

he would often turn to R. C. Trevelyan, elder brother of G. M. Trevelyan, the far more famous historian. R. C. Trevelyan was known, if at all, as a mediocre poet, but he showed critical acumen when he took Forster to task for facetiousness. Many of the early stories and some of the later ones are marred at some point or other by a kind of larky jocularity that, all these years later, sets the teeth on edge.

Two visits, first to Dartmoor and then to relatives in Wiltshire, had him tramping the countryside that he was always to love so much. It was while exploring Figsbury Rings, the Iron Age earthwork between Salisbury and Porton, that he experienced another epiphany and the seed of *The Longest Journey* was planted in his imagination.

At the beginning of the next year, when he was feeling dull, depleted and depressed, he heard through Sydney Waterlow (a diplomatist, a fringe member of the Bloomsbury Group, about whom Virginia Woolf wrote scathingly, when she had seen him bathing, that he looked 'like Neptune, if Neptune were a eunuch – without any hairs, and sky pink – fresh, virginal, soft') of a possible appointment in

'I never saw anybody so incapable', Mrs Forster wrote of her son at about the period when this photograph was taken.

Germany. This was with Waterlow's aunt, Countess von Arnim (the novelist 'Elizabeth' of *Elizabeth and Her German Garden*, later to become the Countess Russell), who was looking for some educated and well-behaved young man to go out and tutor her three eldest children. 'Elizabeth', a cousin of Katherine Mansfield, was the daughter of a businessman who had made a fortune in Australia. At the time of her invitation, she, her husband, her children and a retinue of tutors, governesses and servants were living in a huge *Schloss*, almost a hamlet in itself, at Nassenheide in Pomerania. She called Count von Arnim 'The Man of Wrath'; he might have retaliated by calling her 'The Woman of Whim'. To many who knew her only superficially she was a delightful creature to the day of her death: witty, generous, high-spirited, intelligent, responsive. But there was a mordantly teasing, cruel, steely side to her – revealed, for the most part, only to her dependants. Hugh Walpole was to follow Forster as tutor, in a succession of young men who, almost without exception, left wishing that they had never come near the place. Walpole was a masochist;

and sadists such as 'Elizabeth' detect the presence of masochists and set on them as cats do fledgling birds. She made his life a hell that one can only hope was also pleasurable. She tried it on with Forster (as he amusingly related almost fifty years later in 'Recollections of Nassenheide'), greeting him: 'How d'ye do, Mr Forster. We confused you with one of the housemaids. . . . Can you teach the children, do you think? They are very difficult . . . ah yes, Mr Forster, very difficult, they'll laugh at you, you know. You'll have to be stern or it'll end as it did with Mr Stokoe.' But Forster had an inner strength that poor Walpole lacked and it was not so easy to humiliate him. He refused to be impressed – her false teeth were indifferent and he did not care for her society drawl.

Like his mother during her years as a governess and like his friend Christopher Isherwood, who was to be employed as a tutor of the same kind many years later, Forster found that he would be treated now as a friend and confidant of his employer and now as her servant. The tutors and governesses all ate with the family, though they would no doubt have preferred to eat by themselves; but, as though to remind them that they were present only on sufferance, they were, like commoners in the presence of royalty, not supposed to initiate a conversation but merely to answer when addressed.

Forster made friends with the rather sentimental, rather bossy German tutor and with the various governesses. However much people might bore him or provoke his disapproval, he was adept at presenting a courteous, friendly front. When the Man of Wrath, whose advent had been heralded with so much trepidation, finally appeared, Forster managed to get on well even with him, despite the terrible scenes that he made about the food and despite his habit, odd in an aristocrat, of gargling with his finger-bowl water.

Slowly 'Elizabeth' began to realize, as she realized with Katherine Mansfield, that here was someone too remarkable to be bullied, mocked and patronized from the height of her position and wealth. Forster had met some people who knew her in Dresden. 'They don't like me', she told him. 'Yes, so I saw', he returned demurely. What finally clinched things was the arrival of a number of the *Independent Review* in which there was an article by Forster. She seized it, remarking: 'I'm a very severe critic, I warn you.' When she brought it back, she was 'in a highly chastened mood'. From that moment she accepted him both as a fellow writer and as a kindred spirit, the two of them allies against the dreadful philistinism all around them. He was persuaded to read *Emma* to her and she lent him *Erewhon* – a book that had a profound influence on him. In the paper read to the Memoir Club in the 1930s – to which reference has already been made – Forster said of the Countess that 'To be really liked, to really be liked, is probably her deepest inspiration. . . . It does seem odd that one

should be so anxious to please such a person, for she isn't distinguished and she's always ungrateful. Yet one is anxious, and she will have menials, unpaid and paid, to wait upon her until she dies. To want to be loved does pay.' But the true secret of the hold that 'Elizabeth' exerted even as an old, raddled and far less famous woman, may in fact have lain elsewhere: in the eagerness of people to meet the challenge of someone whose admiration and approval can be earned only with difficulty and may at any moment be withdrawn for the most capricious of reasons.

Forster was patronizing of 'Elizabeth' as a woman; he also underrated her as a writer, as he underrated May Sinclair, an even better novelist, almost his equal. 'Elizabeth's' later novels are shrewd and tart. Nor was she by any means lacking in critical acumen. Having re-read *Howards End*, she commented in her Journal (22 June 1923): 'Disliked first part – disliked his women all through – think it can justly be described as full of promise. He has a curious effect of sidling up to one with his whimsies – then suddenly real power.'

Forster left Nassenheide at the end of that July – probably the most successful and the best liked of all the tutors employed by the Countess because, unexpectedly, he had proved the one least amenable to teasing

Forster with the German tutor, Herr Steinweg, at Nassenheide, 1905. 'Elizabeth' twitted Forster with allowing himself to be 'bossed' by his colleague.

San Gimignano, the model for
'Monteriano' in *Where Angels Fear to
Tread*

'Pope Gregory appearing to Santa
Fina' by Ghirlandaio. In *Where
Angels Fear to Tread*, Santa Fina has
become Santa Deodata: Gino 'gave
candles to Santa Deodata' desiring
'to become the father of a man like
himself'.

and bullying. He returned to England by way of Rügen and the Baltic, in time for publication of his first novel *Where Angels Fear to Tread* by William Blackwood in October 1905. The edition was one of 1,050 copies, increased by a further 526 the following January after some good reviews. The most percipient and the most favourable review of all came from C. F. G. Masterman, for many years literary editor of the *Daily News* and also a Liberal Under-Secretary of State, Home Department. He saw that in the novel Forster is juxtaposing two ways of life: that of 'Sawston' with its 'mediocrity and dulness, and spitefulness and society' and that of 'Monteriano', so intense, easy and free. Here are matched 'worldly success against complete worldly failure, idleness in the sunlight against a beaver-like industry under grey skies, material comfort contrasted with indifference to life's minor luxuries, life lived for the future contrasted with life living on the past.'

Forster's pleasure in the success of this first novel was marred for him only by his nagging relationship with Meredith, who had now taken up a lectureship at Manchester University. In what suggests a manic-depressive disposition, Meredith was now bubbling over with self-confidence and now reduced to a state of apathy and even despair. Significantly, he had no sooner become engaged to be married than he had a nervous breakdown. That engagement was broken off but in no time at all he was engaged again. His imminent marriage must have depressed Forster, who saw himself doomed to relationships in which complete sexual satisfaction was always withheld from him. It was, therefore, a fortunate chance when he was asked to tutor Syed Ross Masood, grandson of Sir Syed Ahmed Khan, founder of what used to

With Syed Ross Masood at Tesserete, Switzerland, where in 1911 Forster confessed his love for a second, still unavailing time

43

be called 'the Muslim Eton'. The invitation came to Forster through two of Lily's friends, Sir Theodore and Lady Morison, who had adopted the Indian as their son near the close of a stay of many years in India. Masood, then and later, was a peacock figure – flamboyant, boastful, self-confident, generous, striking in looks and princely in manner. Forster was captivated. Whether the Indian ever learned much Latin – the subject in which Forster was supposed to tutor him – is highly doubtful; but at least he passed into Oxford and the two men became the closest of friends. That Forster also fell in love, so that that love served to obliterate his love for Meredith, there can be no doubt; but, as so often in Forster's life, there was no hope of physical reciprocation. Masood was soon aware of the other man's feelings for him and seems to have been touched and flattered, rather than repelled.

The Indian had a penchant for telling vainglorious stories of how he had succeeded in putting down this or that member of the British Raj. One such is retailed by Forster in his essay about his friend in *Two Cheers for Democracy*. Masood is outstretched in an empty railway compartment, when a British officer bounces in and orders him: 'Come on! Get out of this!' Masood replies quietly: 'D'you want your head knocked off?' At which the officer exclaims: 'I say, I'm awfully sorry, I didn't know you were that sort of person', and they become excellent friends. Forster adds the proviso: 'Whether this story be true or not . . .' and certainly, like many similar stories in which Masood comes off the victor, it has a factitious air about it. When, some years ago, I asked Forster's friend, Sir Malcolm Darling, what Masood had been like, he replied: 'Oh, good fun, good fun. A bit of an ass.'

Forster was still giving his adult-education lectures when *The Longest Journey* came out in April 1907. In a letter to me, he said that this was the book 'that comes nearest to saying what I want to say'; and he expressed the same opinion on other occasions, both verbally and in writing. It is also, with the exception of *Maurice*, the book that comes nearest to saying what he wants to say about himself and his own life; but, inevitably, because homosexuality was then a tabu subject, because he did not wish to shock his mother and because he was naturally reticent about himself, it is his own story told largely in metaphor. Rickie, for example, like Philip in Somerset Maugham's *Of Human Bondage*, has a club-foot – in his case, significantly, an inherited affliction, as Forster may have suspected that he had inherited his homosexuality from his father. Rickie's mother, dead by the time he is fifteen, is all sweetness and goodness; but the book also contains, as though the author's subconscious were forcing him to express another view of the mother whom consciously he could only adore, the character of Mrs Failing, the sister of Rickie's father. In some ways, in her occasional moments of prophetic wisdom, her occasional acts of spontaneous generosity and her occasional moods of kindness and

Acton House, near Felton, Northumberland, the original of 'Cadover' in *The Longest Journey*

tolerance, she looks ahead to Mrs Wilcox in *Howards End* and Mrs Moore in *A Passage to India*. Yet she is capable of whimsical cruelty, of cold vindictiveness, of heartless contempt. Forster declared that she was based on an uncle of his called Willie; critics have suggested that she was based on Marianne Thornton, another moneybags, or on 'Elizabeth'. But I am convinced that, most of all, even if Forster himself was not aware of it, she is based on his highly ambiguous feelings towards Lily. Then there is Stephen Wonham – a 'blend of pagan god and modern hooligan', as one reviewer of the time described him, 'a kind of Tony Lumpkin' as another did. Consciously Forster no doubt intended Stephen to personify the pagan spirit of the English earth; but, on a deeper level than that, he created him as the fictional embodiment of the ideal partner whom he sought but could not find and for whom he would be willing to lay down his life, as Rickie lays down his life, rather improbably, for the drunken Stephen on a railway line.

The book pleased some reviewers – 'Mr Forster has a future', 'It is a rare achievement to show us the hardest of life's ironies with such intense conviction.' It also pleased 'Elizabeth', who called it 'a wonderful book', adding 'But don't ever marry Agnes', as though that were likely. But there were many reviewers who were puzzled and irritated. The most hostile of these declared *tout court*: '*The Longest Journey* is frankly the most impossible book we have read for many years.' In general Forster's King's friends were unimpressed – a 'dreary fandango' was Lytton Strachey's verdict, for example – even though it was their values, the values of Cambridge, that were so often contrasted favourably with the values of 'Sawston'.

Marble statue of Demeter of Cnidus. 'Demeter alone among gods has true immortality . . . she has transcended sex.' ('Cnidus' in *Abinger Harvest*.) She always remained something of a cult for Forster.

In the summer of 1907, Forster was persuaded to accompany 'Elizabeth' and a large party that included children, friends, ex-governesses and ex-tutors on a caravan holiday in Kent. There were two caravans, each drawn by a cart-horse, and there was also a pony-cart, driven by Margery Waterlow, Sydney's sister. The party assembled in one soggy field, at Crouch, Surrey, and disbanded, before the month for which the caravans had been hired had come to an end, in another soggy field near Canterbury. Surprisingly, Forster enjoyed the discomfort, the gregariousness and even the incessant rain; less surprisingly, 'Elizabeth' did not. The whole enterprise is commemorated in one of her better novels, *The Caravanners*, which had a considerable success in its day.

Early in the next year, Forster was taken by Sydney Waterlow to see Henry James in Rye. James greeted him: 'Your name's Moore' – evidently mistaking him for G. E. Moore. There was tea and conversation about topics as diverse as Queen Victoria's epistolary style (James approved of it), Mary Baker Eddy's financial acumen and Tennyson's reading of his own poems. In retrospect, Forster felt, as one so often feels after such an occasion, that it was an experience that he was glad to have had but not one that he would rush to repeat.

Forster was always a patient editor and critic of his friends' literary productions. He must have needed a great deal of patience to help Julia Wedgwood, a septuagenarian friend of the family, with a revised edition of her history of ethics, *The Moral Ideal*. She eventually rewarded him with £50 – a very handsome sum at that period – and he used this money to travel out again to his beloved Italy for a holiday. Soon after his return *A Room with a View* was published, in October 1908. Though the book is now generally regarded as being slighter than *The Longest Journey*, its reception at the time was warmer.

The following year he had an experience which left its mark on him and to which he would allude from time to time throughout his life, as though he had still not fully worked it out and remained puzzled by it. In this respect, it was akin to that traumatic experience at his preparatory school. He had had dinner with Malcolm (later Sir Malcolm) Darling – now an Indian civil servant, who had been at King's for part of Forster's time there – and with a friend of Darling's, Ernest Merz, also a King's man. Merz – who, in the parlance of the time, might be described as 'a confirmed bachelor' – seemed to be in the best of spirits; but the next day he was found hanged in his chambers. Darling, a man of great wisdom but also of a disconcerting innocence, was more puzzled and less horrified by the incident than Forster, who guessed, no doubt rightly, at some murky secret and, since that secret could so easily have been his own, recoiled.

'The season's great novel' proclaimed the *Daily Mail* of *Howards End*, above a review by the minor novelist Archibald Marshall. 'A fine

A Group of Bathers by Henry Tuke – reminiscent of the epiphany in 'The Sacred Lake' in *A Room with a View*

novel' proclaimed the *Graphic*. 'A story of remarkably queer people' proclaimed the *Western Mail*. The reviewer for the *Chicago Tribune* declared 'My impression is that the writer is a woman of a quality of mind comparable to that of the Findlater sisters or to May Sinclair.' With this Condition-of-England novel, the fictional parallel to Bernard Shaw's Condition-of-England play, *Heartbreak House*, Forster assumed his place as one of the foremost English novelists of his time. He was only thirty-one. Novelists today mature more slowly.

In the period before the book's publication Forster had been through a trying time with his mother. When she had read the proofs, she really had not known what to think of the whole peculiar business of Helen, Leonard Bast and the illegitimate baby and, worse, she really had not known what the relatives would think of it. Her sense of shock now seems as inexplicable as the first Mrs Hardy's over *Jude the Obscure*. If she had objected for literary reasons, it would have been another matter. Forster's treatment of Helen's seduction showed his pathetic inability to delineate any kind of sexual relationship between a man and a woman – not for nothing did Katherine Mansfield jibe 'I can never be perfectly certain whether Helen was got with child by

The Piazza della Signoria, Florence. In *A Room with a View* the statue of Neptune is described as 'half god, half ghost' in the twilight.

The hay fever had worried him a good deal all night. His head ached, his eyes were wet and red, his mucous membrane generally, he informed her, was in a most unsatisfactory condition throughout. The only thing that made life worth living was the thought of Mrs Maurice Hewlett, from whose works she had promised to read to him at frequent intervals during the day.

It was rather difficult. Something must be done about Helen. She must be told somehow that she is not a criminal offence to fall in love at first sight. A telegram to this effect would be cold and cryptic, a personal visit seemed each moment more impossible. Now, The doctor worried and said that Tibby was quite bad. Would it really be wisest to accept Aunt Juley's offer, and to send her down to Howards End with a note?

Certainly Margaret was impulsive. She did swing rapidly from one decision to another. Running downstairs into the library she cried "Yes, I have changed my mind, I do wish that you would go."

Then Mrs Munt arose. You would have thought she had rehearsed the expedition for years, so competent was she. She even knew the kind of clothes one ought to wear — sombre but not too sombre. Her remark "I think a — PRINT" opens a vista of subtleties. A bonnet implies decision. For one thing it cannot be taken off. It is suitable for weddings, ultimatimums, and funerals. Whereas a hat, however monumental, denotes the open mind, and sympathy with youth. Though inclined to the bonnet, Mrs Munt had also to consider the wishes of her niece. She must not be too decided, too monitory. [And the hat that she acquired, though black on the whole, gleamed iridescently in its more secret parts, as if to]

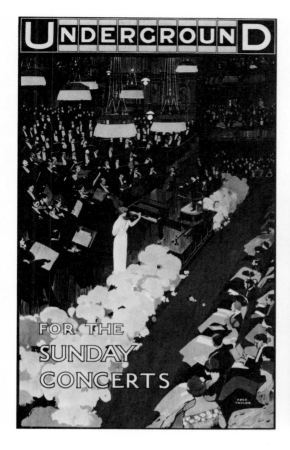

Leonard Bast or by his fatal forgotten umbrella. All things considered, I think it must have been the umbrella.'

So far from the success of the book appeasing Lily, it seemed only to exacerbate her further. Then, at the outset of the next year, Forster's maternal grandmother, the much-loved Louisa, died. Since, with the longevity common to the Whichelos, she was eighty-three at the time, Lily's anguish seemed to be out of all proportion to her loss. When suicides leave notes, the reasons they give for killing themselves are not always the true ones; and similarly, on a smaller scale, when people give way to depression and self-reproach, as Lily now did, the true reasons are not always those that they give to others or even to themselves. Lily had allowed herself to be adopted by Marianne Thornton and to that extent she might have some slim grounds for guilt; but all that had been a long, long time ago. It seems more probable that her state of turmoil had quite another cause: her growing realization of her son's true sexual nature and her jealousy because of it. Forster's love for Meredith, a fellow undergraduate, could easily have been dismissed by

Left: Underground poster, showing the interior of the old Queen's Hall – scene of the concert in *Howards End*

Right: All Souls Church, Langham Place, by Charles Ginner. 'Your house at All Souls Place somehow suggested the Schlegels' house for me.' (Forster to G.L. Dickinson, 1931)

Opposite: Manuscript sheet of *Howards End*. 'I am grinding out my novel into a contrast between money and death' he reported at a moment of discouragement.

49

Illustration from the *Graphic*, 1908.
'The bride and bridegroom drove off
yelling with laughter.' (*Howards End*)

her as the kind of intense but manly friendship so common at a period
when women were excluded from so many areas of male life. But
Forster's love for Masood – an Indian and a pupil of his – would less
easily admit of disguise or self-deception.

However little he desired it – and for all his life he was to remain
genuinely reclusive and shy – the success of *Howards End* made Forster
into a public figure. This, too, his mother appeared to resent, seeing
their intimacy threatened by a host of importunate strangers or near-
strangers, with their invitations to parties and literary meetings and
their requests for lectures and advice. It was now that Forster moved
from the periphery of the Bloomsbury Group to a position nearer its
centre; with the consequence, among other things, that he sat for the
well-known Roger Fry portrait. As Florence Barger told the story, this
used to hang in Lily's drawing-room until a visiting clergyman peered
at it and then, alarmed, asked her: 'Your son isn't queer, is he?' Lily at
once removed the portrait, which she had never liked anyway, and it
was passed on to the Bargers.

Every aspiring writer who prays to God for success should add the
proviso 'But not too much, O Lord, and not too soon!' Forster had

now had success in full measure and he had had it at an early age. The weight of people's expectations became a ball-and-chain on his creativity. He began a novel, *Arctic Summer*, and then, having completed a few chapters, gave it up. He wrote some of the pornographic stories that did so little to enhance his reputation when they appeared after his death. He produced some reviews. Partly because of this lack of a strong imaginative impulse, partly because of his frustrated love for Masood and his longing to see him again, but no doubt also partly because he wished to get away from his mother, Forster now began in 1912 to plan his first passage to India. He was to set sail in October of that year with R. C. Trevelyan and G. H. Luce, another Cambridge friend, who was on his way to take up a job in Burma. Goldsworthy Lowes Dickinson, who had been awarded one of the first Albert Kahn Travelling Fellowships, joined the boat at Port Said. The Anglo-Indians (I use the term in its former sense of English people working in India) hardly knew what to make of the quartet, as they compared Dostoyevsky with Tolstoy loudly in public and lolled around instead of joining in all the planned sport and festivity. 'No doubt we did look queer', Forster himself admitted; and this queerness earned them the nicknames of 'The Professors' and 'The Salon'.

Left: Florence Barger, with her son Evert

Right: Portrait of Forster by Roger Fry

A guest of Lady Ottoline Morrell
at Garsington Manor, *c.* 1922–3

Below, Julian Bell and Roger Fry,
painted by Vanessa Bell

Opposite, top: Lytton Strachey holds
court at Garsington Manor,
surrounded (*left to right*) by Lady
Ottoline Morrell, Maria Nys (later
Mrs Aldous Huxley), Duncan
Grant and Vanessa Bell.

Below left: with T.S. Eliot. When,
on Eliot's seventieth birthday,
Forster was approached by Neville
Braybrooke to contribute to a
celebratory anthology, he declined
on the grounds that 'I am not
sufficiently in sympathy with his
[Eliot's] outlook.'

Below right: Saxon Sydney-Turner
by Vanessa Bell, *c.* 1913. Virginia
Woolf wrote of the 'exquisiteness' of
his nature, though she found that
his chronic melancholia infected her.

Outside the Club.
Lucknow.

'Turtons and Burtons' outside the
Club, Lucknow

Having arrived in Bombay, the friends split up: Luce to go on to
Burma; Dickinson and Trevelyan to go to the caves of Ajanta and
Ellora; and Forster to be reunited with his beloved Masood, who was
now in Aligarh. Unfortunately he and Masood rarely had a moment
of privacy together, so many were the relatives and friends and hangers-
on who were always crowded about them. After a week in Aligarh
and another week in Delhi, where they were the guests of a Muslim
doctor friend of Masood's, Forster went on alone to Lahore to stay
with Malcolm Darling and his wife Josie. Though the Darlings were
themselves liberal in their attitude to the Indians, it was now that
Forster first came into wholesale contact with his 'Turtons and
Burtons' – he had already met a Mrs Turton on the boat – and
conceived the resentment that eventually resulted in his blanket
condemnation (with the exception of the Darling-like Fielding) of all
the British in India in his novel. Peshawar, Simla and Agra followed –
Dickinson and Trevelyan joined up with him at the last of these, as
they had done at Lahore and at Peshawar – and then Gwalior, where,
on apologizing for keeping an elephant waiting, Dickinson received
the lordly answer 'Elephants sometimes wait four hours.' Now came

54

the most interesting part of the tour for him: a stay in Chhatarpur as a guest of the Maharajah Singh Bahadur, who was later to figure so amusingly and so touchingly in J. R. Ackerley's *Hindoo Holiday*. Forster described the Maharajah as 'a tiny and fantastic figure, incompetent, *rusé*, exasperating, endearing'. He was given to asking questions like 'Tell me, where is God? Can Herbert Spencer lead me to him, or should I prefer George Henry Lewes?' As Ackerley, with characteristic frankness, revealed in *Hindoo Holiday* and as Forster, with characteristic delicacy, shrank from revealing in his life of Goldsworthy Lowes Dickinson, the Maharajah was a pederast, forever in search, like Ackerley, of the Ideal Friend.

His companions now moved on to China, while Forster continued to zigzag about the northern half of the subcontinent. Through the Darlings he became both the guest and the friend of the twenty-four-year-old Maharajah of Dewas Senior, a Mahratta of unprepossessing looks and unimpressive size, who none the less was to exert a profound influence on Forster, so that he was later, in the preface to the book that he wrote about the state (*The Hill of Devi*), to call his stays with him, now as his guest and later, in 1921, as his private secretary, 'the great opportunity of my life'. Apart from another reunion with Masood – two weeks of further longing and frustration – the most important event to follow was a visit to the Barabar Caves, which were to become the scene of Adela Quested's ambiguous ordeal.

Entrance to one of the Barabar Caves – originals of the 'Marabar' Caves in which Adela Quested suffers her equivocal ordeal

Edward Carpenter saw the 'Uranian man' as someone 'by no means effeminate' and himself dressed and behaved accordingly.

On his return from India, one of the most momentous meetings of Forster's life was to take place. This was with Edward Carpenter, at the house which he shared with his working-class lover, George Merrill, at Millthorpe. Forster had, of course, already read Carpenter. Indeed, Carpenter's influence on him had been far more pervasive than that of G.E. Moore or the Bloomsbury Group. With Carpenter, Forster believed in 'Love, the Beloved Republic' (the phrase derives from Swinburne's 'Hertha'); and, like Carpenter's, Forster's was a non-revolutionary kind of Socialism that exhorted 'Rend your hearts and not your governments.' Forster, when he came to write about Carpenter, tended to be patronizing – as one so often is about those who have influenced one far back in the past. But he had to admit that he was 'possibly great', even if 'his heart was stronger than his head'.

Carpenter had written about Beethoven in a book, now long forgotten, called *Angel's Wings*: and when we read in it of an Arietta that is 'like the unfolding of a child's face, like the carol of a lark, like the sunlight on the sea', etc., we are at once reminded of that embarrassing passage in *Howards End* when the third movement of the Fifth Symphony is interpreted in terms of goblins 'walking quietly over the universe, from end to end'. Carpenter, too, had been at Cambridge, writing of it: 'This succession of athletic and even beautiful figures, what a strange magnetism they had for me, and yet all the while how insurmountable for the most part was the barrier between.' He had, prefiguring Forster's maxim 'Only connect', repeatedly stressed the need for man to establish a unity of body and spirit. Carpenter had taken holy orders and then, sickened by what he had regarded as a betrayal of his inmost nature, had given it all up – the Church, orthodoxy, the middle-class values in which he had been nurtured – and had gone to live and work with manual labourers.

'I was perhaps too intellectualised and mentally fidgety quite to suit him', Forster confessed; but Carpenter exerted over him, at least during the early years of their friendship, 'the influence which used to be called magnetic, and which emanated from religious teachers and seers'. At the third of Forster's visits, an incident, slightly comic and yet fateful, took place. Carpenter's beloved, George Merrill – a rough, tough 'working-class bloke from the slums', so ignorant that, when he heard that Gethsemane was the place where Jesus had slept on his last night, he asked in all innocence 'Who with?' – touched Forster's backside – 'gently and just above the buttocks'. In his account, Forster goes on: 'The sensation was unusual and I still remember it. . . . It seemed to go straight through the small of my back into my ideas, without involving my thoughts. If it really did this, it would have acted in strict accordance with Carpenter's yogified mysticism, and would prove that at that precise moment I had conceived.'

The result of this immaculate conception was the novel *Maurice*, which Forster began to write in 1913, finished in 1914 but continued to tinker with at intervals, up to his death. He saw no prospect of its publication 'until my death and England's', since unlike Carpenter he was, where his homosexuality was concerned, not one to stand up and be counted but to sit down and be counted out. When Ackerley once took Forster to task about his timidity, saying 'After all, Gide has come clean', Forster snapped back 'But Gide hasn't got a mother.' He seemed to have forgotten that Gide had both a wife and daughter. In addition to scruples about his mother, Forster also felt that to publish the book would somehow damage his image as 'the Sacred Maiden Aunt of English Letters, Keeper of the Bloomsbury Conscience' (as Cyril Connolly characterized him).

André Gide, by Paul Albert Laurens

W.J.H. Sprott, Gerald Heard,
Forster and Lytton Strachey in the
early twenties

It was Connolly who put most vividly and succinctly the reason
why, when the book at last appeared in 1971, it was greeted with a
certain embarrassment by even Forster's most ardent admirers. Yes, it
showed 'the quality of a novelist at the height of his powers' but

by now the element of dating is fatal, like foxing on a book. It's not all that
important, but one can't ignore it. We can make allowances for what dates if
it was once contemporary, even as the foxed pages were once immaculate, but
there's something artificial where a book is born dated.

Carpenter saw the book soon after its completion and declared
himself 'very much pleased with it'. Lytton Strachey wrote a
devastating letter, in which he put his long and bony finger on exactly
what many people, homosexuals no less than heterosexuals, have felt to
be wrong with the central relationships. 'I really think the whole
conception of male copulation in the book rather diseased.' He then
refers to the 'speechification by which Maurice eventually refuses to lie
with Alec on the last night. . . . It is surely beastly to think of
copulation on such an occasion – shall we copulate? shall we not?
ought we to? etc. – All one can think of is that one must embrace.'
Forster was a life-long and self-confessed onanist and there is something
overwhelmingly sad about his masturbatory fantasy – as about most
masturbatory fantasies – of finding happiness in the arms of some
brawny and inarticulate son of toil. It is the mirror-image of the

romantic fantasy of a novelist like Ouida, in which the girl from a 'modest' background is swept off her feet by an Old Etonian guardee, a peer or a *principe*. The only point at which Strachey was wrong was when he described the relationship between Maurice and his Mellors as 'a very wobbly affair; I should have prophesied a rupture after 6 months.' After all, Carpenter and Merrill remained together for a lifetime, as did Forster's close friend, William Plomer, with the faithful working-class man whom he loved.

Critics have not been slow to point out the parallels between Maurice's love for his game-keeper and Lady Chatterley's for hers. There are as many reverberations from Carpenter in Lawrence's work as there are in Forster's and it is largely these reverberations that produce the similarities in the attitudes to human existence of two otherwise such dissimilar novelists. Both, with Carpenter, deplore what industrialization has done to destroy the countryside and its culture and believe passionately in what Lawrence called 'the spirit of place'; both assert the overriding importance of personal relationships and distrust movements that seek a change of political forms rather than of hearts; both believe in a 'blood-consciousness' which enables people to communicate on a level beyond words, as Mrs Moore and Professor Godbole communicate with each other in *A Passage to India*.

At first the two men got on well together. At the beginning of 1915 Lawrence, pursuing Carpenter's dream of a fellowship of like-minded souls, had begun to plan 'Rananim' – 'a little colony where there shall be no money but a sort of communism . . . a community which is established upon the assumption of goodness in its members, instead of the assumption of badness'. Forster was to be one of the members, along with Middleton Murry 'and our women'. In fact, the only kind of community that Forster would ever have dreamed of entering would have been either a monastery or (as he did later in his life) an exclusively male college. The idea of his mucking in with Frieda Lawrence, Katherine Mansfield and Lawrence's female disciples would have at once been seen as preposterous by anyone not of Lawrence's *naïveté*.

However, Forster disqualified himself before long, when he visited the Lawrences in the cottage that had been lent to them by Viola Meynell in Greatham, Sussex. First, he upset them by retailing 'a ghastly rumour' to the effect that the police were about to intervene to stop the sale of *The Prussian Officer*. After this inauspicious start he got increasingly on their nerves. Writing, after Forster's departure, to Mary Cannan, wife of the novelist Gilbert Cannan and previously wife of J. M. Barrie, Lawrence told her: 'We had E. M. Forster here for a day or two. I liked him but his life is so ridiculously inane, the man is dying of inanition. He was very angry with me for telling him about himself.' The anger is not surprising: Lawrence's home truths, like those of

Max Beerbohm caricature of Lytton Strachey, 1931

James Sleator's portrait of Forrest Reid – to whom Forster once said: 'The only thing in daily life that seems to you beautiful *in itself* is school, friendship.'

'Elizabeth', could be sadistic. Lawrence also wrote to Bertrand Russell about the visit – 'we were on the verge of a quarrel all the time.' There follows some kindness of a patronizing kind – Forster has 'something very real in him if he will not cause it to die' – but much more contempt. Why can't Forster take a woman and 'fight clear to his own basic, primal being'? He 'sucks his dummy . . . long after his age'. In the ensuing months Lawrence's remarks both about Forster and to him became increasingly rebarbative, until Forster deliberately withdrew from any further intimacy. Frieda undoubtedly helped to exacerbate the differences between the two men, as so often between Lawrence and his friends. On one occasion Forster received from Lawrence a letter over which Frieda had scrawled her comments. This evoked from him the dry comment that he would 'have no dealings with a firm'.

A more serene and lasting friendship that began at this same time was with the Belfast novelist Forrest Reid, about whom Forster was later to write a perceptive essay, published in *Abinger Harvest*. Forster had written Reid a fan-letter after reading an early novel of his, *The Bracknells*, and Reid had then responded with praise for *The Celestial Omnibus* and *The Longest Journey*. Forster followed this up with a visit to Reid in Belfast, where Reid led a simple life in the company of his dogs and cats and the boys whom he befriended. An extremely ugly man, he was a pederast who, like many pederasts, perpetually harked back to the lost heaven that had lain about him in his boyhood. He is usually represented as having been happy and uncomplicated; but in fact his was a dark, involuted, troubled nature and in the course of his life he made more than one attempt at killing himself. When, as inevitably happened, the boys whom he loved grew up, had girlfriends and got married, he indulged in scenes of bitter recrimination and maudlin self-pity.

Reid's characters are convincing only when they are either themselves youthful or in love with youth. But within this restriction he is a remarkable and strangely underrated writer. If one sets a descriptive passage by Reid against one by Forster, it is nearly always Reid – so lucid, so limpid, so totally without affectation – who comes out the better. The two men, though so different, instantly took to each other. Forster described Reid, in his furry tweeds and heavy brown boots, as 'un-Londony'; which may have been part of his attraction for him, just as Forster's cosmopolitanism may have been part of his fascination for Reid. On Reid's occasional visits to London – he would usually cross the Irish Channel only if he were to play in a round of croquet matches – he would stay with Forster for a night or two, and the two men would then indulge in such unsophisticated pleasures as visits to the Science Museum, the London Zoo or Whipsnade. Once Reid asked Forster to try to get him admission to the Black Museum at Scotland Yard. One of his best novels, *Following Darkness*, was dedicated to Forster soon after their first encounter. Forster, more in joke than in earnest, then suggested that he should also dedicate to him the novel that followed it; but Reid did not oblige.

Unlike the Woolfs, Lytton Strachey and some other Bloomsberries, who were able to go on with their day-to-day lives – entertaining each other, gossiping about each other, worrying about their reviews, complaining about the difficulties of finding domestic servants, as though a terrible holocaust were not taking place less than a hundred miles away from them – Forster was unsettled and depressed by the war. Visiting Goldsworthy Lowes Dickinson in Cambridge in 1915, he witnessed a scene that, though superficially trivial, brought home to him the 'obscenity' of what was taking place. A solitary undergraduate in cap and gown walked around a corner and was confronted by a group of young Welsh soldiers. The soldiers burst into laughter. 'They had never seen anything so absurd, so outlandish. What could the creature be? To me the creature was the tradition I had been educated in, and that it should be laughed at in its own home appalled me.'

For a while Forster worked as a cataloguer in the National Gallery, while many of its treasures were being put away in safety; then in November 1915 he left for Egypt, where he was employed by the

Preliminary sketch of Forster by Sir William Rothenstein

International Red Cross until January 1919. Before his departure he was interviewed by Gertrude Bell – 'scholar, poet, historian, archaeologist, art critic, mountaineer, explorer, gardener, naturalist, distinguished servant of the State', as the Introduction to her *Collected Letters* describes her – and no doubt intimidated by such a plethora of qualifications, by her statuesque presence, by her disdain for appearances ('Her clothes and colours were always wrong', T. E. Lawrence was later to write of her) and by her authoritative manner, Forster was jumpy and subservient. As a reaction, when he later had to submit to an interview with a senior official of the Red Cross, he was 'uppish and impertinent at the wrong moment (it's called initiative when it's at the right moment)' and only slipped through by the skin of his teeth.

Alexandria during the First World War, as during the Second, contained a cosmopolitan community of homosexuals, who were little bothered by the restraints of the law or by barriers of class or nationality. Forster soon made a number of congenial friends and lost some of his more obtrusive old-maidish traits, of the sort that never ceased to irritate the wholly masculine Leonard Woolf. At first he put up in a modest hotel; then through a fortuitous meeting with an American widow, he became a lodger in the house of the widow's retired Greek maid. Tolerant and kindly, she became a kind of mother-figure to him; but one whose demands were less exacting than those of Lily. 'Under her relaxing sway, I gave up wearing my uniform except for my duties, and slid into a life that suited me and into a variety of acquaintances who never coalesced into a set.'

Those duties were not too demanding. When Forster had arrived in Alexandria, a Turkish invasion was threatened and he had been, as he put it, 'in a slightly heroic mood'. But that threat had passed and the mood had passed with it.

What had begun as an outpost turned into something suspiciously like a funk-hole, and I stuck in it for three years, visiting hospitals, collecting information and writing reports. 'You are such a wonderful *sticker*', a detestable Red Cross colonel once said to me scathingly. I was; and I dared not retort that it takes both stickers and climbers to make a world.

In June 1916 there was a scare that he might be called up – and in Egypt there was no provision for conscientious objectors to appear before tribunals, as many of his Bloomsbury friends had done in England. Fear of being called up also prevented him from going home on leave, much though he wished to see his mother and she to see him.

Apart from the major work of this period, the charming and scholarly *Alexandria, A History and a Guide* (written while in Egypt but not published until 1922), Forster also wrote the articles gathered into the slim volume *Pharos and Pharillon* and, in addition, an astonishing

A coin of Antoninus Pius (AD 138–61) showing the famous lighthouse in Alexandria, one of the Seven Wonders of the Ancient World, erected by Ptolemy II

number of other articles, most of them ephemeral and of little value, for the *Egyptian Mail*. In his book on Forster, Lionel Trilling says that this was the period that gave Forster 'a firm position on the Imperial question'; but his friendships with Leonard Woolf, Goldsworthy Lowes Dickinson and Masood, and his travels in India, had already given him this, so that the behaviour, past and present, of the British in Egypt only confirmed existing judgements. When, in 1920, a lengthy pamphlet, *The Government of Egypt: Recommendations by a Committee of the International Section of the Labour Research Department*, was published, it included 'Notes on Egypt' by Forster, in which he gave a careful account of British exploitation and bungling (as he saw it) in Egypt, as a prelude to the Committee's recommendation that the British should withdraw as soon as possible from the country.

Forster's duties for the Red Cross were not all that dissimilar to those of Walt Whitman during the American Civil War. But, perhaps predictably, though he was attracted by many of these working-class soldiers, mutilated, in pain or homesick, he could experience none of Whitman's passionate self-identification with their sufferings. To Bertrand Russell he wrote: 'I love people and want to understand them and help them more than I did, but this is oddly accompanied by a growth of contempt. *Be* like them? God, no.'

The Red Cross Hospital, Alexandria, during the period of Forster's attachment

In wartime Alexandria – 'costumed in khaki'

Opposite: Mohammed⁄el⁄Adl, Forster's Alexandrian beloved. The facial resemblance to the young Bob Buckingham is pronounced.

It was now, in 1916, that at last Forster found total sexual fulfilment – or, as he put it, 'parted with respectability'. After that he made other experiments; until, in 1917, he fell in love with a tram⁄conductor, Mohammed⁄el⁄Adl, with whom he had a relationship that was both deeply satisfying and potentially dangerous. The two of them could not be seen together either on tramcars or in places frequented by the British. He sent the man's photograph to Florence Barger back in England – she had by now become his confidante, the only female one he was ever to have – and she lent it to Carpenter, who commented: 'But what a pleasure to see a real face after the milk⁄and⁄water, mongrelly things one sees here! It was a literal refreshment to me. Those eyes – I know so well what they mean, and I think you do too, *now*!' Strachey was, perhaps predictably, more cynical – might not Forster be making rather too much of the whole affair? After leaving

Egypt, Forster kept up with Mohammed and even saw him again in 1922, when he was returning from India. But the Egyptian's health was giving way and Forster sadly acknowledged that, though he had often thought of spending the rest of his life with him, that had been only a dream. The differences were too great, the difficulties too formidable, there was a wife. Not long after, the Egyptian died.

Next to this, the most important friendship of these years – though it was never an intimate one – was with the Alexandrian poet C.P. Cavafy. To Forster belongs the credit of having first introduced him to the English-speaking world through an essay in *Pharos and Pharillon* and of having subsequently acted as the poet's unpaid agent, publicist and adviser. Cavafy returned that debt by giving countless leads for the guidebook and, in a less tangible but no less valuable form, by refining and deepening Forster's sensibility through the medium of his poetry. In his *Pharos and Pharillon* essay, Forster brilliantly evokes a casual meeting with the poet in the streets of Alexandria, as he is 'going either from his flat to the office, or from his office to the flat'. One hears one's name 'proclaimed in firm yet meditative accents – accents that seem not so much to expect an answer as to pay homage to the fact of

C.P. Cavafy, of whom Forster wrote that 'he can give the sense of human flesh and blood continuing through centuries that are supposed to be unsatisfactory'

Opposite: The salon of Cavafy's 'dusky family-furnished flat' in rue Lepsius, Alexandria

66

individuality' and there, as one turns, 'is a Greek gentleman in a straw hat, standing absolutely motionless at a slight angle to the universe'. If Cavafy is going to the office, then he vanishes after his greeting; but if he is going home, then 'he may be prevailed upon to begin a sentence – an immense complicated yet shapely sentence. . . . Sometimes the sentence is finished in the street, sometimes the traffic murders it, sometimes it lasts into the flat.' This flat was in the rue Lepsius, an ill-lit and ill-famed street, and Cavafy was usually at home to his friends between the hours of five and seven. He was at that time working for the British in a minor post in the Department of Irrigation. Though his salary was modest, the poet was generous with his whisky, even if he had two classes of it – the better for the people whom he genuinely liked and respected, the worse for the droppers-in and scroungers. In a letter to Cavafy's biographer, Robert Liddell, Forster has described how he would return with the poet to the dusky, over-furnished red salon or to the larger Arabian salon with its Oriental-looking furniture, each lit by candles or a petrol-lamp if night had fallen, and would there try to make out the poems with his recollections of Ancient Greek and the aid of George Valassopoulos's translations.

'You cannot possibly understand my poems, my dear Forster . . . impossible,' and then he began to lead me through one of them, *The City*, I think, and: 'But good – my dear Forster, very good indeed – you have seen the point . . . good.'

In an unpublished draft, Forster noted down a further recollection of those evenings in the rue Lepsius:

It never occurred to him that I might like his work or even understand it. . . . When he was pleased he'd jump up and light a candle, and then another candle and he would cut cigarettes in half and light them and bring offerings of mastica with little bits of bread and cheese, and his talk would sway over the Mediterranean world and over much of the world within.

Mr Liddell recounts how, on one occasion, a literary group who called themselves The Apuani suddenly burst in, some twenty of them, on one of these sessions. 'Cavafy was much annoyed but kept his temper, introducing them to Forster in the most complimentary terms.'

Unlike Forster, so generous of praise to the writers whom he admired or liked, so willing to promote them, so eager to enhance their reputations, Cavafy was egocentric where writing was concerned. He would flatter his literary visitors if, by doing so, he thought that he would advance his own reputation, but he disliked rivalry and was, therefore, loth to encourage others in creative work. Over the years Forster did a great deal for him: urging the dilatory Valassopoulos to proceed with his translations; later encouraging Cavafy's other translator, John Mavrogordato; bringing Cavafy to the attention of editors in England; introducing his work to poets as diverse as T.S. Eliot, Siegfried Sassoon and Robert Graves; seeking advice on how best to achieve publication of the poems in England. But Cavafy took little interest in Forster's own work; there is no indication that he even bothered to read the novels. The correspondence of the two men after Forster's departure from Alexandria is concerned almost exclusively with Cavafy and Cavafy's literary career. Such generosity of spirit is not common in writers and it does Forster credit.

These were happy years for Forster. 'Middle-aged people ought to go away and get other experiences', he wrote, as a very old man, in a *Listener* article. By going away, freeing himself from Lily and plunging into a passionate love-affair, he seemed to have escaped from that 'inanition' diagnosed by D.H. Lawrence and so began to prepare himself, after an unsettled and unsettling interval between the completion of *Howards End* and *Maurice* and his departure from England, for the triumph of *A Passage to India*.

On his return to England at the beginning of 1919, he worked briefly and unenthusiastically as literary editor of the Socialist *Daily Herald* and once again began to contribute essays and reviews to a variety of periodicals, most of them left-wing, like Leonard Woolf's *The Nation*. When he received a renewal of a long-standing invitation to go out to India once again, as temporary private secretary to the Maharajah of Dewas State Senior, who had entertained him on his previous visit, he accepted with alacrity. There was much that he wished to escape in England; and he wished to see Masood again. Sir Malcolm Darling, who had been tutor to the Maharajah, described Dewas State Senior and its neighbour, Dewas State Junior, as 'the oddest corner of the world outside *Alice in Wonderland*' – a plateau 2,000 feet above the sea where two rulers each had his own palace and court and army and national anthem, and where two little principalities not merely existed side by side but even intermingled, with one state owning one side of a street and the other state the other. The Maharajah was a touchy, intelligent, capricious man, given to sudden enthusiasms and sudden fits of despair. Forster thought him 'certainly a genius and possibly a saint, and he had to be a king'. The English officials who had to cope with his rapidly changing moods may not have all concurred in that flattering judgement. Forster got on well with him even if he also felt that, ignorant of the language and unskilled in administration, he was really inadequate for the job.

Masood came for a visit of three days. He rather threw his weight about, no doubt because 'his descent from the Prophet was better documented than that of the Maharajah from the sun' and because his employer, the immensely rich Nizam of Hyderabad, was far more exalted than this little princeling. Accompanied by clerks and files, he was censorious of the administrative inefficiency he saw around him. Not unnaturally, Forster is indulgent in his account; but it is easy to see that Masood's lofty behaviour must have been something of a trial to his hosts.

Forster's duties were not dissimilar from those of a wealthy woman's 'lady companion'. He would read aloud to the Maharajah (Matthew Arnold and Macaulay were two of the authors favoured); play cards with him; supervise the gardens, tennis courts, Guest House, 'Electric House' and cars; open all letters; and, most important of all, be available to receive the Maharajah's confidences at any hour of the day or night. On his own initiative he founded a Literary Society but it soon fizzled out. For the most part he was happy; but there were times when the muddle and mess began to depress him – 'there is no dignity, no taste, no form' he wrote to his mother – and felt that 'Though I am dressed as a Hindu, I shall never become one.'

He was involved in two dramas during his stay. In each case, the cause was absurdly trivial but the echoes reverberated on and on, becoming increasingly magnified, as in those caves in *A Passage to India*. In the first, English insensitivity grated against Indian oversensitivity, leaving a sore place that soon went septic. The agent to the governor-general for Central India arrived on a ceremonial visit. *Attar* and *pan* were proffered by the members of the agent's party to the Maharajah's entourage. Forster, being in an ambiguous situation, an Englishman in the private employ of an Indian, was somehow overlooked. This was an Insult and the Maharajah forbad him to have anything more to do with the English visitors. Later, the prime minister of the little state was bidden to draft a protest to the agent. Two months afterwards, when Forster was in Simla with the Maharajah for a conference of rulers, the Insult had still not been forgotten: the whole story had to be told yet again to Sir John Wood, the political secretary to Lord Reading, the viceroy.

The second drama, no less worthy of inclusion in *A Passage to India*, concerned a colonel whom Forster calls 'Wilson' in *The Hill of Devi* but whose real name was Leslie. It was for this elderly and slightly absurd Englishman that Forster was acting as stop-gap private secretary to the Maharajah while he was on leave. Before his departure the colonel had been planning an elaborate garden; but, in doing so, he

Forster in Indian costume, looking as though he were wearing one of Aunt Rosie's hats

Group at Dewas State Senior, showing the Maharajah and his son (*front row, centre*), with a mighty memsahib rearing up between them

had omitted to provide for any kind of irrigation. When he heard that, at the advent of the hot weather, this area had become a desert, he was extremely upset. What would happen if the Prince of Wales were to include the state in his forthcoming tour and find that the palace and its grounds had become 'a dung-hill and a rubbish-heap'? There would be nothing for the colonel to do but cut his throat at the shame of it all. Obviously the old gentleman was unwell and overwrought. He began to suspect Forster of intriguing against him in order to usurp his job; and when, imagining that they were concerned with business, Forster opened some letters to the colonel that had in fact been written by a female correspondent, the fat was truly in the fire. The colonel wrote an insulting missive – 'I know that some people feel when they get east of Suez that not only the ten commandments are obsolete but also the obligations and etiquette of English society.' Forster, surprisingly, answered almost as pompously and childishly. In the event, though Forster did not stay on in the job beyond the agreed term – he had no wish to do so – the colonel did not return to it. The

The Hill of Devi, which gave the title to Forster's Indian memoir

Maharajah decided that after 'this middle-class row' (as Forster termed it) he did not want back his former employee.

Before leaving India Forster had another meeting with Masood. The frustrated passion that he had felt for the Indian on his pre-war visit had now modulated into no more than an affectionate admiration.

During his stay at Dewas, Forster had written regularly to his mother, to other relatives and to Florence Barger and it is these letters that not only made up the major part of *The Hill of Devi* (not published until 1953) but also provided a rich store of material for *A Passage to India*. The whole last section of the novel, 'Temple', derives from his attendance at the eight-day Gokul Ashtami Festival in honour of Krishna – 'rites in which a European can seldom have shared', as he himself described them in *The Hill of Devi*.

Forster had been working on *A Passage to India* before this 1921 visit and he had hoped to continue with it while he was in Dewas. But the chapters already completed seemed to 'wilt and go dead' when he was back in the country that they were supposed to describe, so that he felt 'only distaste and despair' when he took them out and looked at them. Once back in England, he found himself able to continue; but even now there were many occasions when he all but gave up. He found himself bogged down in the worst such impasse when he came to the end of the second section of the novel and had to begin on the third,

'Temple'. His eventual solution, for all the virtuosity of the writing, is thin and shaky: a piece of canvas covered with a brilliant *trompe-l'œil* where the third and final arch of the edifice ought to soar. During this last period of self-doubt and impotence, the sane and sensible encouragement of Leonard Woolf was decisive – without it, he would, as he himself acknowledged, probably never have completed the book. Yet, even as he did so, he felt – as he confided to Virginia Woolf in 1926 – 'This is a failure.'

The friendship of Leonard Woolf meant a great deal to him; that of Virginia Woolf rather less. Apart from his mother, his other female relatives, Elizabeth Poston, Florence Barger and May Buckingham (wife of his closest friend during the second half of his life), he never felt wholly at his ease with women. 'I always feel him shrinking sensitively from me, as a woman, a clever woman, an up-to-date woman', Virginia Woolf recorded in her diary in 1919, after they had run into each other in the London Library. She herself was attracted by his 'transparency and lightness' – she compared him to a blue butterfly – and she respected his judgements of her work, even if they also sometimes irritated or depressed her. In her company, as in Florence Barger's, Forster was under no obligation to maintain a pretence. One weekend for example, when Forster was a guest of the Woolfs, the

Virginia Woolf by Vanessa Bell, 1912

Leonard Woolf and G.L. Dickinson at Asheham House, 1914

three of them began talking of 'sodomy and sapphism' with such frankness that Forster declared the next day that he must have been drunk. Forster told the Woolfs that a famous Methodist preacher of the day, Dr Head, boasted of being able to 'cure' homosexuality and Leonard Woolf then asked him if he himself would wish to be cured. Forster gave a definite 'No' to that but then, surprisingly for one reputed to be so liberal, added that lesbianism disgusted him because he did not care for women to be independent of men.

Yet, in spite of such confidences, there was always a faint discomfort between the two novelists. Virginia Woolf was always highly competitive – when Katherine Mansfield died, though she had been genuinely fond of her, she could not repress the thought, and even recorded it in her diary, that a rival was now out of the way – and she knew that Forster was one of the three novelists of the period (Joyce and Lawrence were the others) who might be regarded as her betters. She would praise his work, as she would praise Joyce's and Lawrence's; but in each of these cases the honey of her praise always had in it a drop or two of acid. Forster and she came nearest to a quarrel when she wrote two articles about him, one for the *New York Herald Tribune* and the other for *Atlantic Monthly*, in 1927. The tone, especially of the second of these, was intermittently feline and Forster, usually impervious to criticism of his work, was hurt.

With Leonard Woolf, on the other hand, Forster felt completely secure and at his ease. Like Darling, here was a man of grey and gritty integrity, whose essential maleness was never in doubt, and Forster responded to him, as to Darling, like a son to a father. Quentin Bell, Virginia Woolf's biographer, suggests that, in his affection and respect for Leonard Woolf, Forster resented, as Woolf himself did not, the tendency of the world to dismiss him merely as the husband of the famous novelist.

When *A Passage to India* appeared in June 1924, the reception on both sides of the Atlantic was overwhelmingly favourable. J.B. Priestley, a writer whom one would not expect to be in entire sympathy with Forster and about whom Forster could be scathing, summed up the general reaction when he wrote: 'Now that he has come back, as a novelist, to a world that is even more insane and even more in need of his clear-sighted exquisite charity than the world he stopped writing about so many years ago, now that he has returned we should celebrate that event.' A less fulsome note was struck by Edwin Muir, who included in a perceptive review the biting comment that: 'The intellect is not exercised to its utmost in going halfway in all directions.' Middleton Murry, uncannily prescient in a review that rankled with Forster, saw the book as a dead-end – 'the planning of Mr Forster's next novel should carry him well on to the unfamiliar side of the grave.' Murry's reason for this verdict was that Forster seemed to him to have come, like his own Mrs Moore, to 'that state where the horror of the universe and its smallness are both visible at the same time' and, after such a 'twilight of the double vision', what more was there to say?

At the time of its publication, the book was acclaimed both as a triumphant work of art (which it was) and as an accurate delineation of the teeming life of the Indian subcontinent (which it was not). Unlike Maugham, who had travelled the Far East to learn about his compatriots, Forster had travelled India to learn about the Indians. The Muslims are drawn with marvellous skill, the Hindus with only a little less so; but the Anglo-Indians are complete caricatures. The absurdities of the scenes in which the Anglo-Indians are involved range from the farcical elements of the trial scene (the case against Aziz is, for example, conducted by the Superintendent of Police instead of by the Government Prosecutor) to everyone on every occasion, in the original edition, addressing the Collector as 'Burra Sahib'. (Forster was subsequently to make some alterations.) Such ignorance is astonishing. Fielding, the liberal principal of Government College, and the man who in part suggested his character, Sir Malcolm Darling, were, in fact, in no way unique in the India of the time, as Forster seems to have believed. Since the majority of those who passed out top in the civil service examinations of the day opted for the Indian rather than the English civil service, it would be surprising if they had been. After such misrepresentation, my father's story of fellow passengers on their way out to India by boat beginning to read Forster's novel and then chucking their copies overboard in disgust and fury is only too credible.

Tennis party in India

Whether Murry was right in his diagnosis of Forster's spiritual state, he was certainly right in his prognostication about his future. Others, including Forster himself, adduced other reasons for the abandonment of the novelist's role. Lionel Trilling diagnosed 'a refusal to be great'. People less charitable diagnosed the sloth and procrastination that Forster himself characterized as his two besetting vices. When pressed by friends or strangers to give a reason for his silence, he would often reply simply 'I have nothing more to say.' Occasionally he would declare that England and the world had both changed so much that he could no longer embrace them imaginatively in all their 'gigantic horror'. His Commonplace Book shows that, from time to time, he did in fact pursue the possibility of another novel; but he had no wish to be a bore 'from a sense of literary duty', like Thomas Mann – a strange misjudgement of an author whose last novel was so full of vivacity and so amusing.

But Prospero did not break his staff; he merely exchanged it for a walking-stick. The obvious parallel here is with Thomas Hardy – whose work, incidentally, Forster admired, comparing it favourably with Meredith's. Neither novelist abandoned writing, in the manner of Rimbaud; each merely abandoned the art of fiction. But whereas the demands of poetry were even more imaginatively exacting for Hardy than those of the novel, in the case of Forster his biographical and critical essays and books, though he does not deserve Lawrence's dismissal as 'rather a piffler now' for having written them, none the less show a distinct decline. Only he could have produced the fiction; but the non-fiction might have been produced by Lytton Strachey, Harold Nicolson, Logan Pearsall Smith or any one of a number of other elegant, cultivated and accomplished littérateurs of the period.

Having been released from the agonies of being a creative artist, Forster enjoyed the pleasures of being a sage. For many people he was the touchstone of civilized, humanistic values in that period between the two wars that he and others have called the Long Weekend. For every one person whose life was changed during those years by a reading of the novels, there must have been ten whose lives were changed by a reading of the non-fiction.

Among the famous who urged him over the last half-century of his life to return to the novel was Beatrice Webb, who asked him in a letter why he did not write 'another great novel . . . giving the essence of the current conflict all over the world between those who aim at exquisite relationships within the closed circle of the "elect" and those who aim at hygienic and scientific improvement of the whole of the race?' Presumably she placed Forster and the Bloomsberries in the first category and herself and Sidney Webb in the latter. The idea was not a bad one; but it did not stimulate Forster to take up his pen. Years later, T. E. Lawrence urged him to write a 'mucking-about-the-town-with-

Charles Mauron, who might have been described by Bloomsbury as 'our man in France'

common-men book'. One shudders to imagine what that suggestion, if acted on, might have produced.

It was in April 1922, soon after he had returned from India, that Forster initiated what was to prove one of the most important friendships of his life. He had seen in the *London Mercury*, a poem, 'Ghosts', by an unknown writer, then in his twenty-sixth year, called J.R. (Joe) Ackerley and had been so much impressed by its 'combination of the reminiscent and the dramatic' that he had written a long fan-letter. In later years Ackerley was not to think much of the poem – 'not a very worthy midwife' for their friendship, he decided. The two men eventually met at the 1917 Club in Gerrard Street, Soho – its membership took in politicians of the left and the Bloomsbury intelligentsia – and at once liked each other. Ackerley, who had served in the war and had then gone up to Cambridge, was at an unsettled period of his life, when he was trying to write but having little success in doing so. When Forster mentioned that his old friend the Maharajah of Chhatarpur was looking for a secretary, Ackerley jumped at a suggestion that was eventually to result in a book, *Hindoo Holiday*, even more entertaining and vivid than Forster's own *The Hill*

of Devi. Before Ackerley sailed, Forster kept flooding him with advice: he must keep his stomach warm if he was to avoid diarrhoea; he should not demand his return fare in advance as that might create a bad impression; he had better engage and pay his bearer himself, as the man would then be 'wholly under your thumb'. With a change of roles, it was a curious re-enactment of the solicitude displayed by Lily before Forster's own two passages to India.

The two men corresponded at length during Ackerley's five-month absence, with the younger titillating his mentor with 'crafty-ebbing' (Forster's pun) accounts of the doings of the homosexual Maharajah. When Ackerley returned to England the following year, they began to see each other regularly. Ackerley at that period was a man of outstanding good looks – though the suggestion, sometimes made, that he and Forster were lovers for a time is without foundation. Since he was also tall, well-built and without any trace of effeminacy, he could be frank about his sexual proclivities with little likelihood of open derision or hostility. On the rare occasions when he met with these, his attitude was, to put it vulgarly in an expression he favoured, 'Arse-holes to you!' In all this he was very different from the man whom Virginia Woolf described as 'timid as a mouse'.

Opposite, above left: J.R. Ackerley and his sister Nancy, one of the great beauties of her day

Opposite, above right: At Monk's House

Opposite, below: Forster and J.R. Ackerley (*extreme right*) with pals on Chiswick Reach

In *A Room with a View* George 'followed Freddy into the divine' when he entered the pool that the Honeychurches called 'The Sacred Lake'. George was naked; Forster is here decorously clad.

Drawing of Forster by Edmond Kapp, 1930

Much of Forster's sexual life was conducted either furtively or in his imagination – which, in later years, he sustained with books dealing with the ever-interesting topic and with his friends' accounts of their exploits. Here Ackerley was invaluable. During the 1920s and 1930s he lived, by his own admission, a life of extreme promiscuity. So feverish was the hunt for the Ideal Friend whom, tragically, he never found except in canine form, that, travelling to some appointment, he would jump off his train or bus long before his destination had been reached, in order to pursue a distant face, a fleeting smile, a disappearing pair of shoulders or buttocks. This recklessness fascinated the prudent Forster. Just as, when young girls go out together, they often come in one plain and one pearl, so, when homosexuals are close friends but not lovers, the same pattern is often noticeable. Ackerley was the bold, attractive, matey one of the partnership; Forster the one who was timorous, dowdy and unassertive.

As so frequently in such relationships, the plain one had on occasions to cover up for the pearl. On his way out to India Ackerley had pursued an Italian sailor on the boat and had had a brief affair with him. Much later there was an opportunity to join up with him again in Turin and Ackerley, not wishing to arouse his father's suspicions, persuaded Forster, who was usually truthful, to conspire with him in 'a thumping lie' and to pretend that, instead of being far away in the embrace of his Italian, he was in the bosom of the Forster family in Weybridge. Unfortunately, while Ackerley was away, his father had a heart-attack, which it was feared might prove fatal. A telegram was dispatched to Weybridge; and Forster then had the disagreeable task of travelling over to the Ackerley home in Richmond and confessing to the deception.

When Ackerley was living at No. 6 Hammersmith Terrace in 1925, he was hailed one evening by a policeman, Harry Daley, who had recognized him as the author of the recently produced play *The Prisoners of War* – which, because of its homosexual theme, had had to be put on at a theatre club. An intelligent, decent and kindly man, Daley became a life-long friend both of Ackerley and of Forster, often visiting Ackerley's rooms with his mates from the police station. As Ackerley put it, 'He got me going socially in Hammersmith much faster than I could have got by myself.' Through Daley, Ackerley met another policeman, Bob Buckingham, and in the course of events introduced him to Forster, thus drastically changing both men's lives. Curiously, despite the evidence of correspondence, Forster would like to maintain in later years that it was *he* who had first met Buckingham and had then introduced him to Ackerley.

In a personal memorandum, dated 1935, Forster confessed: 'I want to love a strong young man of the lower classes and be loved by him and even hurt by him. That is my ticket. . . .' Once he had broken through the barriers of repression and guilt in Alexandria, he achieved at least the first part of this wish on numerous occasions. In 1925, for example, it was a Weybridge bus-driver called Tom with whom he was infatuated. Writing to Ackerley, he described how their nine hours of lovemaking had been terminated only by the imminent parturition of Tom's wife. Over the years Forster was to expend a great deal of money on people like Tom. It is easy to assume an attitude of moralistic disapprobation about these affairs; but given the economic situation of the time and given the sexual tolerance of the working class, so much greater than that of the middle class, it is priggish to do so. Forster derived a great deal of pleasure from these affairs, however transitory; and his partners were glad of help to pay doctors' bills, settle overdue rent demands and take the children to the seaside.

Unlike Ackerley, whose relationships tended to be tragically short and who had neither the means nor the will to be financially generous, Forster would continue to see and, in many cases, help to support his former lovers and their families long after all sexual attraction had vanished. Thus he still kept up with H. O. Meredith, even though he had long since begun to find him tedious and depressing. ('He is always saying that nothing and no one is of any use, and I think, as I have always thought, that he is right, but he says it so slowly that the impressiveness of the truth vanishes and nothing survives but the boredom.') Similarly, for many years he maintained an unbroken friendship with Frank Vicary – 'miner, fisherman, ship-steward, torpedoed, miner again, pig-breeder' – through a life littered with tragedies and disasters. Just as Forster had helped Daley when the policeman, in those days before the National Health Service, had wondered how he would be able to pay for a major operation for his mother, so he was constantly coming to the aid of Vicary, his wife and his children – one of whom was christened 'Morgan', much to Lily's disgust. When the eldest child died, Forster went down to visit the family in the country, in an effort to console – the kind of action that is always more difficult and more useful than the sending of a letter or a cheque. Forster thought that Vicary had more than talent as a writer – 'Poor old Frank has genius in him, you know, Joe, a lot, and you have a bit and I have none', is his surprising declaration in a letter to Ackerley – and he spent a great deal of time encouraging him in his writing and trying to make others of his literary friends encourage him. As the years went by, until Vicary's death in 1956, it is clear that it became more and more of a duty and less and less of a pleasure for Forster to see him; but still he persevered to the end.

Far more rewarding was the friendship with Buckingham and his family. When Forster first met him in 1929, he was a man of striking looks, in a dark, masculine manner. There is a story of a luncheon meeting in Paris between Gide and Forster, to which Forster took

H.O. Meredith, of whom a disillusioned Forster wrote in later years: 'To turn a hero into a jolly old boy is a ghastly task.'

along Buckingham, uninvited, in the mistaken belief, so common among homosexuals, that the friend whom he found so attractive would prove equally so to his host. Buckingham was not of the type that Gide admired; and since he could speak no French, the conversation limped along. Gide never felt quite the same towards Forster, even though, at his death, Forster actually wept.

In later years Forster often took Buckingham and his wife, May, abroad on holidays with him (Buckingham had by now left the police force to become a probation officer); stayed with them on innumerable occasions; and helped with the education of their son, Rob. When this son, their only child, died of Hodgkin's Disease in 1962 at the tragically early age of twenty-nine, leaving behind him a widow and two boys, each of whom had been given 'Morgan' as a second name, Forster at once provided a monthly allowance by deed of covenant so that the home of the young family should not be broken up. The widow, Sylvia Buckingham, has put on record: 'He saved me a great deal of financial strain, worry and anxiety.' Such acts of generosity and kindness were common in his life; they were often performed anonymously.

At the end of 1924 and the beginning of 1925 Forster was taken up with a move from the house, Harnham, Monument Green, Weybridge, in which he and his mother had made their home for the last twenty years, to a house the lease of which he had inherited from an aunt. This, the only house in existence designed by his father, was West Hackhurst, Abinger Hammer, near Dorking. Lily was now at an age when any change upset her and she was reluctant to make a move, even suggesting that they might keep on both houses; but her hand was 'gently forced' (as Florence Barger put it) by her son. In order to feel free to carry on his increasingly eventful private life without his mother's prying or disapproval, Forster from now on also maintained a London perching-place – first at 27 Brunswick Square, London W1 and later, in order to be near the Buckinghams, at 9 Arlington Park Mansions, Sutton Lane, Chiswick.

Life in the Victorian house at Abinger Hammer went on with a matching Victorian formality and amplitude. Before dinner, a maid would bring to the Morris-papered bedrooms brass cans of hot water, which she would set on the marble-topped washstands, having first covered each with a towel. So far from having running water in the

West Hackhurst, originally named Laura Lodge when it was designed for Aunt Laura by her brother, Forster's father

The entrance to the Chiswick block of flats in which Forster had his London *pied-à-terre*

bedrooms, the house did not even have a bathroom. The maid always wore the black uniform, white apron, starched cuffs and cap of an already obsolescent calling. There was a gardener called Bone, who was subject to minor accidents. When William Plomer went to tea, he marvelled at the silver spirit-kettle and the old-fashioned cake-stand. When the Woolfs went to dinner – they were in a hurry and had to eat faster than Lily could have approved – all the family silver was out and candles illuminated the table. In such surroundings, it is not surprising that Forster should have written to Ackerley before a visit to admonish him not to discuss 'cock-stands'. The admonition was a joke, of course; but Ackerley, who believed in always being himself, could easily have brought up the subject and, such was his charm, might even have got away with it.

It was through Ackerley that Forster first came to broadcasting. One of the earliest of his talks was given with Buckingham in February 1932, with Ackerley, who had not yet become literary editor of *The Listener*, acting as producer. The title was 'Conversation in a Train'. A novelist (Forster) meets a policeman (Buckingham) for the first time and by accident in a train. Each asks the other some rather ingenuous questions about his job – How does the novelist create his characters? Why don't people in general like the police? One senses that Forster was less concerned with producing an interesting broadcast than with partnering Buckingham in a joint endeavour.

After the completion of *A Passage to India* Forster had intensified his activities in journalism. In April 1924 he served, rather improbably, as the special correspondent of the *Nation and Athenaeum* to the Empire Exhibition at Wembley. He wrote only two despatches, summing up his impressions: 'Millions will spend money there, hundreds will make money, and a few highbrows will make fun. I belong to the latter class.' But his work never seemed to him so important that he could not be distracted to help or encourage a friend. Ackerley kept getting bogged down in his attempts at creative writing; and since Forster had endured such a predicament often enough himself, he was full of sympathy and advice.

Another writer to whose work he gave endless time and thought was 'the little fellow who is labelled for posterity as Lawrence of Arabia'. 'With the flair that he had shown when seeking patrons in the world of Power' (as one of his biographers, Desmond Stewart, puts it), T.E. Lawrence decided that, along with Bernard Shaw and Edward Garnett, Forster was to be one of the editors of his *Seven Pillars of Wisdom*. In fact, it was the non-professional, Charlotte Shaw, who probably did Lawrence the greatest service by telling him, surprisingly, when he himself was on the point of losing his nerve, '*Don't leave out the things an ordinary man would leave out:* the things people will tell you are "too shocking"'; but Forster comes a close second to her. There is a remarkable modesty in a letter which he writes to Lawrence before they have met each other and sets down his qualifications for telling him what to do: 'Have written some novels, also done journalism and historical essays; no experience of active life, no power of managing men, no Oriental languages, but some knowledge of Orientals.' There is also a remarkable combination of toughness and tact in his lengthy comments on the book.

Eventually the two men met and, from a certain coyness on the one side and a certain archness on the other when they subsequently corresponded, it seems indisputable that Forster was attracted by Lawrence and that Lawrence was aware of the attraction. When in 1928 Forster's collection of short stories, *The Eternal Moment*, appeared, it carried an ambiguous dedication 'To T.E. in the absence of anything else'. This was because one of the published stories 'The Point of It' was 'a feeble timid premonition of the one which is with you now and which is yours really' – that story being 'Dr Woolacott',

'Private Shaw' (T.E. Lawrence) by
Augustus John

one of those that appeared only after Forster's death, in which a
Lawrence-like stranger returns from the grave to bring both life and
death to a Forster-like invalid. In his Memoir of Lawrence, Forster
writes of meeting him by chance at a concert at Queen's Hall
(destroyed in the Blitz), in the company of men 'whose faces I
instinctively distrusted. (All his friends will agree that he had some
queer friends.)' Yet, for all his disapproval, those faces and what they
represented were no doubt some measure of Lawrence's attraction for
him. On 4 May 1935 Forster wrote to Lawrence to suggest that he

might stop with him for a few days at his retreat at Clouds Hill and suggested 20 May as a possible date. On 13 May Lawrence died from injuries received in a motor-cycle accident. For a time Forster was to edit his letters; but he eventually withdrew because of the possibility of libel, against which the Lawrence trustees were not prepared to offer an indemnity.

In 1926 Forster accepted an invitation to give the 1927 Clark Lectures at Cambridge and opted to speak about the Novel. The style was so informal – 'ramshackly' was Forster's own word for it – that A. E. Housman, having attended two lectures, decided to attend no more. As a young man, Forster, like many homosexuals of his day, had felt a community of spirit with Housman, as with Whitman. Reading *A Shropshire Lad* in those days before the First World War, 'the warmth of the writer's heart seemed unalloyed' to him. He was now to learn, on paying a courtesy call on Housman, that that heart was, in fact, singularly chilly. Other people, both when the lectures were delivered and when they were printed, were more appreciative – though, perhaps predictably, Virginia Woolf's review was not wholly favourable.

Forster's attitude to the erosion of liberties during the twenties and thirties seems even more relevant now than then:

We can't build as we like or drink when we like or dress as we like. . . . We can't say what we like – there is this legend of free speech but you try it on: free speech and saying what you want to say are very different things. . . . We cannot go where we like. Escape is impossible. We can only get out of England on a ticket of leave, issued if our conduct is satisfactory. . . . This ticket of leave is called a passport.

Though he thought it right that the law should prevent people from being corrupted, he did not think that it should try to prevent people from being shocked.

This concern for freedom of expression led Forster to agree to appear as a witness in the *Well of Loneliness* case in 1928. 'With a mixture of mortification and relief' he learned that literary evidence would not be allowed and therefore left the court without having had to disobey Radclyffe Hall's injunction that he must declare her novel to be not only serious in intent but also a great work of literature. Many years later, in 1960, he was to give evidence for *Lady Chatterley's Lover* – a work for which he had a scarcely higher regard. Eliot had avoided giving evidence 'from the highest motives' (as Forster ironically put it in a letter) but, victory having been won, he was 'now finding them not so high. All perfect.' Forster could not fail to see the joke of his 'sweating', a very old man, to help someone who had so often treated him with asperity and contempt. 'By the way, did Lawrence ever do anything for anybody?' he asked in that same letter.

Though he was never prepared to 'come out', his attitude to homosexuality became increasingly frank over the years. This process is illustrated by three incidents, one in the thirties, one in the forties and one in the fifties. The first is the successful prosecution of James Hanley's partly homosexual novel *Boy*. Forster did not offer to appear as a witness, along with such writers as A. P. Herbert, H. G. Wells and J. B. Priestley, but privately he expressed admiration for the book and his anger that legal proceedings should have been instituted. The second is the publication of a letter by J. R. Ackerley in *The Spectator* of November 1942, after a 'witch-hunt' in Abergavenny that had ended in one successful suicide and two attempts at it. Forster was not prepared to sign this letter but he gave Ackerley considerable help with its drafting. The third was an article, 'Society and the Homosexual', which he wrote for the *New Statesman and Nation* in 1953.

Una Lady Troubridge and Radclyffe Hall with their dachshunds at Cruft's, 1923

The Memoir Club, by Vanessa
Bell, 1943. Forster *right foreground,*
next to Quentin Bell

His timidity about the subject in the twenties is also illustrated by
his refusal to write a preface for Ackerley's *Hindoo Holiday*. Forster gave
as his reasons that he thought the book too good to need a preface and
that he did not wish to compromise himself over the Maharajah. But
Ackerley realized that the true reason was that Forster shrank from
being associated with what, by the standards of those times, might be
regarded as improprieties and, in consequence, provoking his mother's
disapproval.

During the years of Nazi persecution of the Jews, Forster often
spoke out about racial prejudice – even if he was also capable of
writing back from Frankfurt, where he had been on a visit in 1928 to
see an ailing Syed Ross Masood, that it was 'a lumpy, sallow city,
carpeted with Jews'. Militarism he also denounced on a number of
occasions, even disapproving of the two minutes' silence on Armistice
Day. Yet, as a very old man, he came up to London in order to attend
the Royal Tournament with Ackerley and, after it was over, to repair
to a nearby pub frequented by soldiers, sailors and airmen who had
taken part. This was presumably a case of hating the sin but loving the
sinners.

Sometimes, though he hated violence ('Be soft, even if you stand to get squashed', he once admonished, when considering and rejecting the argument for a Communist revolution), the voice of this parlour radical became strangely shrill. Thus, during the miners' strike of 1926, he was asking 'Ought not the coal-owners to be strung up before negotiations begin?'

He was similarly human in his inconsistency about class. He frequently spoke out against class prejudice; yet, having heard Ackerley recount his experiences with a working-class lover, he later wrote, 'Your troubles have been a great expense to me, for I was so put off the lower classes that I changed my 2nd return for a 1st and enjoyed every inch of the journey in consequence.'

Above: Max Beerbohm caricature of Forster, 1940

Left: By Vanessa Bell, *c.* 1940

In his middle years

The common view of Forster during these years as a retiring and
donnish figure is not in the least borne out by his activities between his
abandonment of fiction and the approach of extreme old age. To write
letters, articles and petitions about minority rights, the destruction of
the countryside, penal reform, the menace of Nazism and Stalinism,
censorship and a host of other issues, was not enough for him. He was
also prepared to join societies, appear on platforms, attend congresses,
sit on committees. Twice, in 1934 and again in 1942, he became
president of the National Council for Civil Liberties. He also served
as president of the Humanist Society.

In 1934 he published *Goldsworthy Lowes Dickinson*, a life written
with more affection than candour. He drew effectively on letters and
his own memories; but he prudently ignored the sexual revelations –
Dickinson might best be described as a 'poderast' – provided by a then
unpublished autobiography.

The year 1936 saw the publication of the collection *Abinger Harvest* and at once Forster was involved in libel proceedings over one of the essays in it, 'A Flood in the Office'. He mentioned the affair to only one or two of his friends but none the less it weighed on him, particularly as he was just recovering from a prostate operation. Many years before, when he had been in Alexandria, two distinguished engineers, Sir William Willcocks and Sir Murdoch MacDonald, had had an unseemly and farcical row about how the waters of the Nile should be treated. Sir William had fired off a broadside at his opponent in the form of a pamphlet, which had been the basis of Forster's original piece in *The Athenaeum* in 1919. Subsequently, unknown to Forster, Sir Murdoch had instituted libel proceedings against Sir William and had won his case. By republishing his article, Forster and his publishers had now reactivated the libel. Eventually, there had to be an apology in court, the payment of damages and costs, and the removal of the offending pages. This will explain why one page of the 1936 reprint of the book bears the eccentric pagination '277–281' and why, though 'A Flood in the Office' appears in the list of contents, the reader will look in vain for it.

In 1935 Ackerley was appointed literary editor of *The Listener*, and for the next twenty-five years, until his retirement from a post that he held with so much distinction, much of Forster's literary journalism appeared anonymously in the Book Chronicle of that journal. Forster did not approve of anonymity and the money to be earned by such work was meagre. It says much both for his modesty and for his love for Ackerley as a friend and his respect for him as an editor that he was content, month after month, to work for him in this way. Ackerley once remarked that his three most valued contributors in the days of *The Listener*'s anonymity were Edwin Muir, Christopher Isherwood and Forster. All three were completely professional, writing exactly the number of words required of them, never being late with copy and never failing to return their proofs. All three, despite their eminence, were never riled if he suggested an improvement.

Though the routine at West Hackhurst often caused him to sigh and groan – his mother had been 'fatigued and fatiguing', the gardener had cut his hand on the shears, the maid had decided to give notice for no reason that was clear to them and Ackerley must come down to find out what lay behind it – Forster entered into the life of the village and its surroundings with evident pleasure. That life was very different from the predominantly intellectual one of King's or the predominantly homosexual one of London or Dover – where he would retreat for holidays in the company of such friends as Air Commodore L. E. O. (Leo) Charlton, author of a number of books for boys, and William Plomer. Typically, on such holidays, he would stay, not in a hotel, but in a modest rented flat.

Forster and Vaughan Williams discussing the Abinger Pageant with the bandmaster. Vaughan Williams remarked: 'I look like a rich and wily cattle-dealer . . . getting round a simple rustic' (Forster).

Opposite: Map of Abinger, 1937

For the village he collaborated with Tom Harrison, founder of Mass Observation, as producer and Ralph Vaughan Williams as composer, in the staging of the Abinger Pageant in July 1934. Its theme was one close to the heart of all three men: the gradual obliteration of the countryside and its culture under the spreading poison-ivy of urbanization. Since by then Forster was generally regarded as the leading British novelist and Vaughan Williams as the leading British composer, an effort that might otherwise have rated no more than an adulatory review in the local press received wide publicity. Its successor, *England's Pleasant Land,* put together by the same distinguished trio and performed at Milton Court, Westcott, Surrey, in July 1938, received even more, with *The Times* according it half a column.

Inevitably the advent of war distressed and unsettled Forster. 'I believe we had to fight this war, yet am doing nothing to win it', he wrote on one occasion; and on another, 'I am afraid that our immediate job, for those of us who can do it, is to suffer.' Florence

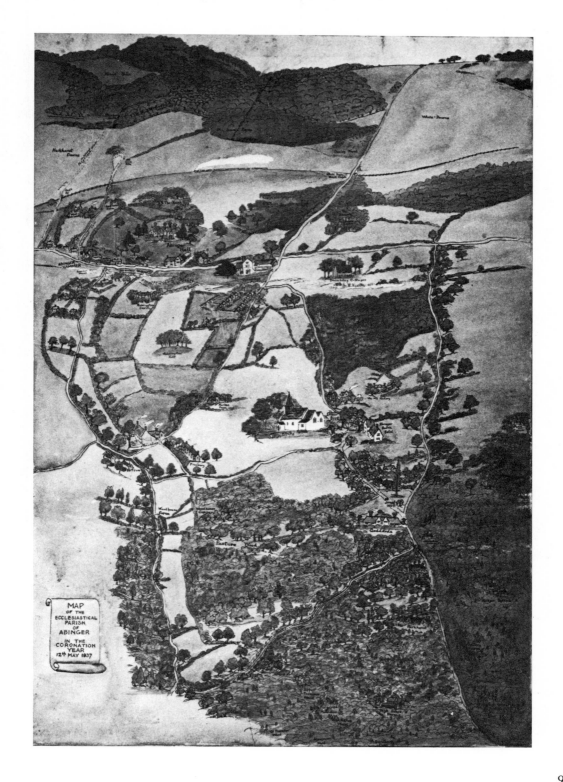

MAP
OF THE
ECCLESIASTICAL
PARISH
OF
ABINGER
IN THE
CORONATION
YEAR
12ᵗʰ MAY 1937

Florence Barger, in active old age

Barger was bombed out of her home in September 1940 – fortunately she and her family were all away at the time – and she then spent a year and a half at West Hackhurst with the Forsters. But there, too, the tranquil life of pre-war years had been upset first by the advent of refugees and then by sirens and even bombs. Lily, crippled by rheumatism and now rarely venturing beyond the immediate neighbourhood of the house, was increasingly demanding. She still, in her late eighties, ran the household, the domestic staff now having dwindled to a single elderly, faithful maid. When at home, Forster spent much of his leisure time either in the garden or in the adjoining wood, which he had bought some years before to prevent its being built on and which, typically, he refused to close to the villagers, who used it for their picnics and as a short-cut to the downs.

His 'war-work' consisted of writing a pamphlet *Nordic Twilight*; of drawing attention to any case of civil liberties being needlessly whittled away on the pretext of 'national security'; and of broadcasting for the BBC – usually on the Eastern Service to India. George Orwell had been his first producer for his monthly, quarter-hour Indian talks; then the poet and journalist John Arlott took over. Arlott has described how Orwell advised him, 'Forster is no work at all; but don't try to alter him.' As when he reviewed for *The Listener*, Forster was the complete professional. His time-length rarely erred by more than a few seconds either way and he had soon grasped the fact that the rhythms, vocabulary and word-patterns of speech must all be different from those of writing.

Through these years he distracted himself with either writing new homosexual stories or tinkering with those already written. Versions were sent out to friends, who were asked for their comments. Many years later, in 1965, Ackerley asked me if I would read a story by a friend of his and tell him frankly what I thought of it. It seemed to me intolerably arch and coy; then suddenly a terrible thought came to me – Could it possibly be by Forster? Ackerley confirmed my suspicion: 'Yes, E.M.F. the perpetrator. . . . I suggested publication to him some weeks ago and he was quite shocked. . . . "I'm afraid I'm a coward."' That story has never been published and presumably was destroyed. I only wish that, where the other facetious stories were concerned, his friends had been firmly discouraging, instead of indulgent. *The Life to Come* and *The Other Boat* are another matter; they are masterpieces of the genre.

Forster was a loyal adherent of PEN, the International Association of Poets, Playwrights, Editors, Essayists and Novelists, both because he regarded it as standing for 'the creative impulse which existed before nationality was invented and which will continue to exist when that dubious invention has been scrapped' and because he had an admiration and affection for its general secretary, Herman Ould. He attended a number of international congresses and himself presided, in the place of Storm Jameson who was ill, at the conference held in London in 1944 to commemorate the tercentenary of the publication of Milton's *Areopagitica*. He made a moving plea at this conference for a minimum of secrecy in public affairs once the war was over – 'How can we try to improve the world when we do not know what the world is like?' sums up his argument. When, in 1946, it was proposed at a Congress of International PEN in Stockholm that a blacklist should be drawn up of writers who had collaborated with the enemy in the war, Forster spoke out bravely in opposition. He had himself been on the Nazis' blacklist.

It was PEN that took Forster on his last visit to India in 1945. By then, Masood was dead, as was Iqbal, a poet whom Forster greatly

With Frank (Frankie) Franklyn at Rooksnest Farm, 1949. He had played with him at the age of five and visited him often in the years between.

97

admired – 'one of the two great cultural figures of modern India', the other of course being Tagore. Naturally, as the author of *A Passage to India* and as the man who, during the war, had agitated on behalf of Jayah Prakash Narayan, the nationalist leader who had been gaoled in Lahore, Forster was received everywhere with affection and respect. But none the less he was sometimes saddened. The Indians seemed to him to be inordinately concerned with politics, politics, politics. 'When I spoke about the necessity of form in literature and the importance of the individual vision, their attention wandered. . . . Literature, in their view, should expound or inspire a political creed.' The poverty was still omnipresent and, since he was now older and therefore less resilient, it depressed him far more than in the past. Travelling by train, he found the vista unrolling beside the window 'monotonous, enigmatic, and at moments sinister'. Even the educated Indians spoke English worse than when last he had been there. 'Did I do any good?' he asked wearily at the end and then decided that, yes, he did. 'I wanted to be with Indians, and was, and that is a very little step in the right direction.'

In India, 1945, from where he wrote: 'I have had the advantages and luxuries of being distinguished, and with the disadvantages . . . I must put up.'

In March 1945, Lily Forster had died. Though she was ninety, she might have lingered on much longer, had she not fallen twice from the bed in which she by then spent most of her time. Florence Barger noted: 'In those last anxious weeks, all the love and tenderness that Morgan felt for her was fully evident.' Yet Forster's announcement of his bereavement to Ackerley is strangely brutal: 'My mouldy mother, as you once called her, is dead, and I now expect to start mouldering myself, in accordance with the laws.' Forster's life had been so much dominated by Lily that many of his friends feared that this process of mouldering would be a rapid one, now that the sun at the centre of his universe had been extinguished forever. As a child, Forster had been in the habit of saying that, when he was grown up, he would marry his mother. In effect, he fulfilled that promise and their life together was similar to that of countless married couples, one important factor excepted. Even in his sixties, he had no sooner arrived from Abinger at the Reform Club or the home of one of his friends than he would hurry to the telephone to assure his mother that he had reached his destination. Thirty years before, Virginia Woolf had written of him 'He spends his time in rowing old ladies upon the river' and that, metaphorically, was what he had spent much of his time doing ever since with his mother and his female relations. But though one part of him welcomed this dependence, another part resented it. He would often complain of trivialities at West Hackhurst: his mother had put the typewriter out of service by lifting it wrongly; 'uninterrupted women' and the wireless got on his nerves; the one thing that could always be counted on to make him 'impressive in the home' was if he 'had been seeing a lot of titled people'. Seven years previously he had also written an extraordinary letter to Ackerley, in which he had said of his mother that 'she has been intermittently tiresome for the last 30 years, cramped and warped my genius, hindered my career, blocked and buggered up my house and boycotted my beloved [Buckingham]'. Yet in that letter he also concludes – almost as though he were trying the persuade himself rather than his correspondent – 'I have to admit that she has provided the sort of rich subsoil where I have been able to rest and grow.' One wonders whether, in fact, this rich subsoil, like the rich subsoil of Marianne Thornton's legacy, may not have done him more harm than good.

Rabindranath Tagore

The lease of West Hackhurst had already expired; but, because of Lily's advanced age, the owners, the Farrer family, had generously ignored this. When, shortly after his mother's death, Forster was at last evicted literally, as he had already been evicted metaphorically, from the nest that the two of them had shared for so long, his friends were even more troubled on his behalf. There had been that childhood expulsion from the Eden of Rooksnest; now there was to be another, that could only be as devastating. But, with astonishing resilience,

With his mother – now grown increasingly dumpy and grumpy – at West Hackhurst

George ('Dadie') Rylands

Forster survived both the loss of his home and its guardian. King's College had already elected him a Supernumerary Fellow from 1927 to 1933 and now, at the instigation of George Rylands, an old friend and himself a Fellow, he was elected an Honorary Fellow. He was given a handsome study in Wilkins's building but actually lived with his friend, Patrick Wilkinson, a respected King's don, and his wife in their house in Trumpington Street. To the rooms assigned to him he transported from West Hackhurst several possessions that he particularly valued. The remainder he either sold or gave away to friends. Seven years later, when the Wilkinsons moved into a smaller house, he took up residence in College.

In 1947 Forster paid his first visit to the United States. Ostensibly this was in order to lecture at Harvard University on 'The *Raison d'Etre* of Criticism in the Arts' but what really impelled him to make the journey – a man of sixty-eight not sure if he still had the stamina and receptivity to 'take on' a new country – was the desire to visit a young actor, William Roerick, whom he had first met when he was

In his room at King's College

serving as a corporal in the United States Army in England in 1943. Characteristically, Forster had included in his itinerary – much to its surprise – a small institution, Hamilton College in upper New York State, merely because it had adopted the village school at Abinger during the years of austerity and had supplied it with materials then in short supply. Apart from the pleasure of talking to such old friends as Gerald Heard and Christopher Isherwood, there was also the pleasure of making such new friends as a black sergeant-major met on a train, and a Mexican encountered by chance in Arizona while the young man was cementing a wall for his mother – Forster perched on the wall, while the two of them chatted.

In May 1949 Forster was again back in the States, this time at the invitation of the Academy of Arts and Letters, to which he spoke on 'Art for Art's Sake'. Buckingham accompanied him. Inevitably, he was lionized wherever he found himself, to such an extent that Roerick and his friend, alarmed for the health of this elderly and frail-seeming guest, felt that they must protect them. But Forster made it amply clear that he needed no protection when he dealt decisively with a tiresome American female stranger who kept pestering him to write something for her – 'Any little impression. Even a letter.'

It was during one of these visits that he telephoned Lionel Trilling, author of a pioneering study of his work, to receive what struck him as a surprisingly frigid welcome. Apparently this most perceptive of literary critics had only just realized that Forster was homosexual; and, having realized it, this most liberal of men was in a state of shock.

During this year and the one that followed it Forster worked with Eric Crozier to produce the libretto for Britten's *Billy Budd* – 'my own happiest operatic collaboration' Britten described it. Forster himself used to 'tinkle' at the piano and music plays an important part in most of his novels, from the *Lucia di Lammermoor* scene in *Where Angels Fear to Tread* to the strange little tune sung by Professor Godbole in *A Passage to India*. In addition, there are several Forster essays that deal specifically with musical subjects. Britten was slightly critical of Forster both for his tendency to stress the 'Feeling' of music as against a more rigorously intellectual approach and for his preference for Romantic over Classical music (he made more than one jibe at Mozart, Britten's favourite composer); but, in the early years of their friendship at least,

Forster at Stoneblossom, New Jersey, during his 1949 visit to the States

Forster at work with Benjamin Britten (*in background*) on the libretto of *Billy Budd*

Theodor Uppman, in the role of Billy Budd. Forster thought him 'perfect'.

Britten was full of admiration for Forster's 'deep perception, quick wit, tireless energy . . . and . . . consistent inspiration'.

Forster threw himself into all sorts of problems that had nothing to do with his prose libretto. He is not sure if Piper is right for the scenery – 'I want a ship that looks like one and is not drippy and apocalyptic.' There is also the worry of finding a singer with the voice, the beauty and the air of innocence necessary for Billy Budd himself, until the arrival from the States of Theodor Uppman, 'the perfect Billy Budd', solves that problem. For many years after this collaboration Forster would continue to visit Aldeburgh and it was there that, in 1967, he heard of the death of Ackerley, whom, in the ordinary course of events, he might have expected to predecease. He wept a little when the news was broken to him and then toddled off to bed. The next morning, whether because, his memory now failing, he had forgotten what had happened, or whether because, when one is close to death oneself, the death of another seems an event of no great moment, he was surprisingly cheerful.

J.R. Ackerley

Before his death Ackerley had been chronically short of money as a consequence of his retirement from the BBC. He had, therefore, been secretly negotiating with the University of Texas for the sale of all the letters that Forster had written to him over the years of their friendship. Forster, not surprisingly anxious about letters in which he had revealed so much about his own secret life and the secret lives of others, had made a number of attempts to get them back but Ackerley had successfully foiled him on each occasion. Writing to Herbert Read, Ackerley had explained the situation: 'He [Forster] does not want them to fall into the hands of officialdom. Nor do I want them in his hands, which is what he desires, for I should never get them back again, and I have both a personal and a posterity interest in them.' During the last months of his life Ackerley was haunted by the suspicion that Forster might have learned of what he might regard as an act of betrayal. There is some discrepancy of opinion as to whether, in fact, he ever did so or not. Certainly, when Forster's will was published, it was surprising that his legacy to Ackerley (void, of course, because he had predeceased him) was a mere £500. He had, however, been extremely generous to him in the past.

Britten's genius was ruthless in its voracity. It chewed up what it needed to sustain it and then spat out the bones. When Forster became slow, doddery and forgetful, Britten's welcome to him at Aldeburgh markedly cooled. Forster, who set such store by friendship and fidelity, was upset.

The act of patronage that brought Forster to King's was as enlightened as that which, later, brought W. H. Auden to Christ Church, Oxford. Neither, of course, was a 'writer in residence' of the kind common in American universities and recently introduced over here. As Forster put it, in a Founder's Day speech in 1952: 'I hold no College office; I attend no committee; I sit on no body, however solid, not even on the Annual Congregation; I co-opt not, neither am I co-opted; I teach not, neither do I think. . . .' It would be idle to pretend that he exerted a potent intellectual influence on the university at large but over the years he certainly exerted a civilizing one on his college. This he did, not so much by attending such meetings as those of the Ten Club, as by making himself accessible to anyone who wished to see him. When those who wished to see him were, in the words of Patrick Wilkinson, 'the Rickies of today', he was delighted to encourage them and draw them out, as Wedd and Goldsworthy Lowes Dickinson had encouraged him and drawn him out more than half a century before; but when they were interviewers, would-be biographers or bibliographers, would-be novelists and sweated labourers from the transatlantic thesis industry who expected him to do much of their work for them, he rapidly became fatigued and irritated.

It has become a cliché to say that Forster became more and more famous with every book that he did not write. In December 1949 he was offered a knighthood but decided to decline it – though, having sent off his letter of refusal, he none the less continued to wonder whether he would have chosen to be called 'Sir Edward Forster' or 'Sir Morgan Forster'. In 1953 he accepted the award of the Companion of Honour – though there was widespread comment that it should have been the Order of Merit. The Order of Merit finally came in 1969.

Forster also became richer and richer with every book that he did not write. He was now widely translated, his books maintained a steady annual sale in Britain, and Santha Rama Rau's highly successful stage version of *A Passage to India*, first produced at the Oxford Playhouse in 1960 and then enjoying long runs in both London and New York, brought him in a sum in royalties that astounded him. (Apart from this adaptation, there were less successful ones of *A Room with a View* by Stephen Tait and Kenneth Allott in 1950, of *Where Angels Fear to Tread* by Elizabeth Hart in 1963 and of *Howards End* by Lance Sieveking and Richard Cotterell in 1967.)

Despite a recent fall, Forster, now eighty-four, attended a performance of the dramatized version of *Howards End* at the Golder's Green Hippodrome in February 1967 and afterwards met the cast.

Ackerley has recorded how Forster would say to him: 'Oh, Joe, I've got such a heap of money, would you like some?' But he was by no means unbusinesslike or unworldly, as this may suggest – he knew the value of money and he knew the value of his own work. He was merely generous. He gave Ackerley thousands (literally) to pay off his debts, to travel to Japan and America and to keep going during his retirement from the BBC on what both thought a shamefully niggardly pension. In his article, 'Forster and King's', Patrick Wilkinson refers to innumerable similar 'clandestine generosities'. Florence Barger also testified to Forster's generosity to herself and her family at times of financial stringency.

When he gave away money, Forster's Clapham Sect ancestry would sometimes assert itself. Just as those upright Thorntons had handed out charity in order to 'improve' the poor, so Forster would write out a cheque to a friend in order that he should do what was best for himself, not what pleased him most. Thus, when he had handed over a substantial sum to Ackerley so that he could revisit the Far East and Ackerley then proceeded to blow the money on food and drink instead, Forster was disapproving. That Ackerley might derive greater enjoyment from sitting in Putney pubs than from walking about Japanese temples and gardens appeared to be irrelevant.

No one seeing Forster in these last years would have guessed that he had £25,000 in his current account. William Plomer has given a brilliant description of his appearance:

Incurious fellow passengers in a train, seeing him in a cheap cloth cap and a scruffy waterproof, and carrying the sort of little bag that might have been carried in 1890 by the man who came to wind the clocks, might have thought him a dim provincial of settled habits and taken no more notice of him.

People used to say of Charles Morgan: 'Nobody could possibly be as distinguished as he looks.' No one, Plomer makes plain, could have said that of Forster, quite the reverse.

Forster never believed in spoiling himself. When, as a very old man, he began to suffer from 'cerebral spasms', he was stricken by one when in his flat in Arlington Park Mansions in Chiswick. His kindly neighbour, Mrs Carney, summoned her doctor and made him some egg custards to eat. After a day or two, Forster announced that he was ready to go back to Cambridge. Mrs Carney got the doctor to come again. He at once said that Forster was in no condition to travel but Forster insisted. Finally the doctor said that, if he travelled at all, it must be by car. Forster pooh-poohed such an extravagant notion. Eventually Mrs Carney and the porter helped him down the stairs and he returned to Cambridge by public transport.

The much-delayed Order of Merit (*top*) and the Companion of Honour which preceded it

On an expedition in the foothills of the Alps

He remained astonishingly active into his seventies and even eighties. A typical account of his doings runs: 'In the past week I have been to Segovia, Myra Hess, "Summer and Smoke", "Day of Wrath" and the Cosin Feast at Peterhouse, and expect to finish with "Antigone".' In a reminiscence in *The Spectator*, published after Forster's death, the novelist Simon Raven gives an amusing account of Forster's general aimlessness and sloth, as he witnessed them as an undergraduate. But Raven had evidently forgotten that by that time Forster had already advanced far beyond the age when most men are doing nothing but pottering about their gardens, watching television and reading the newspapers.

When not seeing friends, watching plays or listening to music, Forster now spent much of his time reading. 'Pleasure' seemed to become an increasingly important literary criterion to him; and 'pleasure' was most likely to be found in explicitly or implicitly homosexual fiction in which the characters achieved some reciprocity of happiness. Thus, there was too little 'pleasure' in Ackerley's *We Think the World of You*, much though he respected it for its stoical truthfulness. Among writers whom he especially admired were Walter Baxter (for his war novel

With Donald Windham in
Cambridge, 1960

Look Down in Mercy); Donald Windham (for his short stories); James
Baldwin, William Golding and, of course, his old friend Forrest Reid.
This narrowing of interest tended to distance him from some of the
literary work of importance produced in this post-war period. The
publisher Marion Boyars tells the story of finding herself seated next to
Forster at the High Table of King's. 'What writers of particular
interest have emerged recently?' he asked. 'Have you read Beckett?' she
replied. Forster shook his head. 'No. Is he any good?'

In 1954 his much-loved friend Florence Barger died, after an illness
in which she had been as dead for many months. He was genuinely
grieved – she had been a close friend of his mother as well as of himself
– but his reaction was an unusual one: 'I have suddenly wanted to
think and look at warm obscenities, this has happened to me when
upset all my life, right back to Alexandria.' Even when he was in his
eighties, warm obscenities still had their attraction. When in London,
he and Ackerley would sometimes visit a homosexual coffee-bar called
'The Mousehole' – 'very sad, scenically and publicly', Forster
categorized it, but added that one must not be sentimental for 'it is the
private part and parts that really matter in mice's lives.' Soon after one
of their calls there, the place was raided by the police and its owners
were fined for 'disorderly conduct'. Forster was excited to think that

With Christopher Isherwood at King's

With Tom Coley (*left*) and Bill Roerick (*right*) at King's College, 1969, celebrating Forster's ninetieth birthday

May Buckingham, John Morris,
William Plomer and Forster (*left to
right*)

they had so narrowly escaped having their names taken. To a surprised
visitor, not a close friend, Forster once handed across a magazine:
'Have you seen this?' The magazine, imported from the States, had
little in it but male nudes.

During the last decade of his life Forster had a number of illnesses
that would have finished off anyone with a constitution less resilient.
On one occasion, in 1962, when he had a heart-attack at the age of
eighty-two, it was science, not the heart-attack, that nearly killed him.
The doctors had pumped him full of an anti-coagulant, with the
consequence that, as soon as they had discharged him, his dangerously
thinned blood began to seep through the tissues into his stomach and
he had to be rushed back to hospital for transfusions. A series of strokes
followed with increasing frequency. One of these took place when he
was alone and he lay on the floor all night – a very cold one – until the
college bedmaker arrived and summoned help. His speech would be
affected by these strokes, as was sometimes his sight, and friends would
have to be summoned to act as his amanuenses. When seriously ill, he
would often stay in Coventry with the Buckinghams, where he was
certain to receive every possible attention.

May Buckingham and Forster at Aldeburgh. By now all resentments between them had healed.

Out walking with Bob Buckingham

Forster and Sir John Wolfenden, brought together for the first time in 1958 for the programme 'First Meeting', broadcast in the BBC Overseas Service. Forster admired Wolfenden for his report on homosexuality.

At this period people would often say of Forster, as they would say of L. P. Hartley, that he was 'a sweet old thing'; but in both cases this estimate was wide of the mark. Each certainly had a large measure of sweetness in his character; but each was also extraordinarily tough. I had an example of this toughness when Forster invited Ackerley and myself to have lunch with him in the Senior Common Room of the Royal College of Art, of which he had recently been made an Honorary Fellow, along with Ackerley. 'That wretched Connolly insists on coming here to see me. He wants me to sign some of my books for him.' Connolly arrived, with all Forster's works, pamphlets included, under an arm, and proceeded to make Forster not merely sign but inscribe each as well. Forster, who loathed to sign copies of his books unless he had presented them, scratched away with a weary courtesy. Then the waiter arrived to take the order for drinks. I asked for sherry. 'A double sherry', Forster told the waiter. Connolly also opted for sherry. 'A *single* sherry', Forster said to the waiter, with a just perceptible emphasis. As soon as we had finished our drinks, Forster rose to his feet and said frostily to Connolly: 'I'm afraid that I must now take my friends in to lunch.'

After Forster's death on 7 June 1970 in Coventry – his ashes were scattered over a rose-bed in the Buckinghams' garden, where they were later joined by those of Bob Buckingham – the termites soon got to work on his reputation, as they do when any world-famous writer vanishes from the scene. Their inroads were facilitated by the posthumous publication of *Maurice* (1971) and *The Life to Come* (1972). The intermittent sentimentality of the former and the arch sauciness of many of the stories in the latter disconcerted even some of his most devoted admirers. The whole subject of Forster's homosexuality, previously handled by critics with the same reticence that he himself had brought to it in public, was now discussed at length and with relish. The general consensus was that Forster's long-suppressed sexuality had maimed him as a writer. More than one reviewer quoted from D. H. Lawrence's letter to Bertrand Russell: 'I get the feeling of acute misery from him – not that he does anything – but you know the acute, exquisite pain of cramp', and then went on to suggest that it was this homosexual 'cramp' that had first inhibited him as a novelist and then prevented him from writing novels at all. But given the fact of his homosexuality, it seems to me that the deliberate suppression of any overt reference to it in the writings published during his lifetime caused Forster to write, not with less, but with an even greater intensity. He was obliged to find a whole series of metaphors for his real sexual preoccupations and it is in these metaphors that so much of the power of his writing resides. Unconsciously, the true relationships between Rickie and Stephen Wonham in *The Longest Journey* and between Aziz and Fielding in *A Passage to India* are of course homosexual ones; but because Forster shied away from making that clear, the books have that much more, not that much less, symbolic resonance.

However, it must be admitted that, even by transposition, Forster was incapable of a satisfactory handling of love between the sexes. This explains why, for all its intermittent brilliance, *Howards End*, once so highly regarded, is now seen by many people as the least satisfactory of all Forster's novels, with the exception of *Maurice*. It is a heterosexual novel but one in which the two central heterosexual relationships – between Margaret Schlegel and Mr Wilcox, between Helen Schlegel and Leonard Bast – simply do not work. This is presumably what Katherine Mansfield meant by her famous judgement:

E. M. Forster never gets any further than warming the teapot. He's a rare fine hand at that. Feel this teapot. Is it not beautifully warm? Yes, but there ain't going to be no tea.

But to jump from this conclusion, as many critics have done, and to say that not only was Forster incapable of expressing sexual feeling, but he was also incapable of expressing deep feeling of any kind whatever, is unjust. There is a certain irony that the man who so often accused the British of suffering from an 'undeveloped heart' should himself have been charged with precisely the same ailment. In neither case is the charge merited: feeling and the demonstration of feeling are two

'Morgan did not like dogs (a bad mark!), he was, if anything in the animal line, a cat man . . .'. (J.R. Ackerley: *E.M. Forster*)

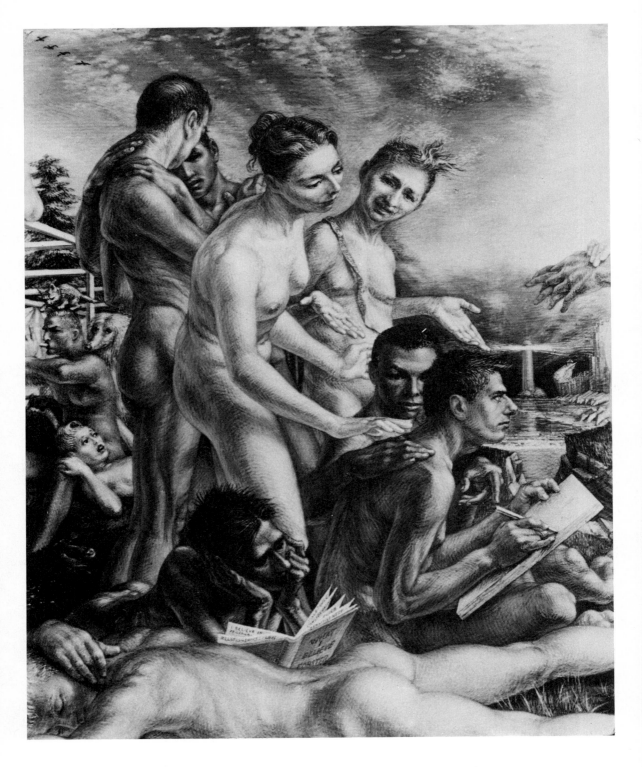

Before appearing as defence witness in the *Lady Chatterley's Lover* case, 1960. 'I had an easy time in the witness-box . . . only made my cold worse and that is better now.'

different things. Just as, in life, an urbanity of manner and a sense of 'good form' tended to conceal from Forster's friends his essentially passionate nature, so in his work an urbanity of style and a sense of literary form have tended to conceal from his critics the essentially passionate nature of his characters' involvements with each other.

At the beginning of 1977 the *Times Literary Supplement* asked a number of the leading writers of the day to name what they considered to be the most overrated and the most underrated literary reputations of our time. Forster figured twice among the most overrated – being named, interestingly, by two writers, Angus Wilson and Anthony Powell, who might be thought to owe a great deal to him. Powell commented that his work 'exuded a smug self-satisfaction' – a charge that might no more unjustly be levelled against Powell's own work. Certainly, when Forster is set beside Mann, Proust or Joyce, or even beside Musil, Gide and Lawrence, he is seen to fall short; but in *A*

Opposite: Detail from Paul Cadmus's painting *What I believe*. Forster, with an uncharacteristic upsticking tuft of hair, is at the back; Isherwood reading in foreground.

Passage to India he wrote one undisputed masterpiece and in *The Longest Journey* he wrote what is nearly one.

Speaking of Edward Carpenter, Forster remarked that 'he is rather forgotten today, partly because he is a pioneer, whose work has passed into our heritage.' The same point was made about Forster in a perceptive piece contributed by Noel Annan to *The Listener* (4 August 1977): 'Paradoxically . . . one of the reasons he no longer speaks to us is that we listened and followed his advice.' In a country in which the bland increasingly lead the bland, we have begun to feel the need for more of those hated and despised 'telegrams and anger' – for more urgency, more passion, not less.

Certainly, in addition to many wise things, Forster also said some astonishingly silly ones. Such, for example, is his extreme statement of his belief that personal relationships are more important than public duties: 'If I had to choose between betraying my country and betraying my friend, I hope I should have the guts to betray my country.' Most of a man's friends are also his fellow countrymen and Forster's preference, if examined logically, is therefore to betray the many rather than the one. An absurdity – unless 'my friend' is a euphemism for 'my lover'. But there was a basic sanity about his judgements, as Virginia Woolf, never a generous critic, appreciated. 'Morgan has the artist's mind', she wrote in her Diary in 1919. 'He says the simple things that clever people don't say. I find him the best of critics for that reason. Suddenly out comes the obvious thing that one has overlooked.'

But, quite as much as the quality of his mind, it is the quality of his spirit that sets him above and apart from most of his literary contemporaries. 'Was he a saint?', Ackerley asks in his little Portrait of him, a question that only a very few of his intimates would ever have thought of putting; and, of course, the answer must be 'No'. He was far too self-aware and far too self-protective to achieve the selflessness of a saint; and, though he disposed of those of his shares that brought him money from such things as armaments or sweated labour, he certainly would never have sold all his worldly goods to give to the poor. But he had about him an indestructible dignity and decency.

What William Plomer called 'the undefinable motive power of his personality, that has put him in revolt against much in his time and enabled him to follow his negatives with a positive creed, attitude, and theory of conduct' seems still, after his death, to have as much force as any of his writings.

Opposite: Portrayed by Cecil Beaton

CHRONOLOGY

1879 1 January, E. M. Forster born at 6 Melcombe Place, Dorset Square, London NW1.

1880 Death of his father from tuberculosis.

1882 Forster and his mother move from London to Rooksnest, Stevenage, Hertfordshire, the original of the house in *Howards End*.

1890 Sent to preparatory school – Kent House in Eastbourne.

1893 Goes as a dayboy to Tonbridge School and he and his mother move from Rooksnest to Dryhurst, Dry Hill Park Road, Tonbridge.

1897 Enters King's College, Cambridge, where he reads first Classics and then History. Obtains a Second in both.

1901 Forster and his mother leave England on a journey that will last a year and take them to Italy and Austria.

1902 Takes a weekly class in Latin at the Working Men's College, Great Ormond Street, Bloomsbury. Goes on a Greek cruise and, near Olympia, gets the idea for one of his best short stories, 'The Road from Colonus'.

1904 The Forsters settle in a flat in Drayton Gardens, London SW10. Forster is now contributing to the *Independent Review*, as well as still teaching Latin at the Working Men's College and also lecturing on Italian art and history for the Cambridge Local Lectures Board.

1905 He goes to Germany as tutor to the children of 'Elizabeth' (Countess von Arnim) at Nassenheide in Pomerania. Publication of *Where Angels Fear to Tread*.

1906 He tutors Syed Ross Masood in Latin and so embarks on one of the closest friendships of his life.

1907 *The Longest Journey* is published. Some praise but reviewers also find it 'difficult' and 'elusive'.

1908 Is paid £50 for helping Julia Wedgwood prepare a new edition of *The Moral Idea*. He uses this money to go to Italy. *A Room with a View* appears. It starts off promisingly but then sales are disappointing.

1910 *Howards End* is published, with such success that at thirty-one Forster becomes a literary celebrity.

1911 Publication of *The Celestial Omnibus*. Sits to Roger Fry for portrait.

1912 Meets Forrest Reid after writing him a fan-letter. Leaves for India, where he sees Syed Ross Masood and visits the states of Chhatarpur ('Chhokrapur' in J. R. Ackerley's *Hindoo Holiday*) and Dewas Senior (later revisited and described in *The Hill of Devi*).

1913 Visits Edward Carpenter at Millthorpe and is touched by Carpenter's friend, George Merrill, with momentous results. Begins to write *Maurice*.

1914 At the outbreak of war, becomes a cataloguer at the National Gallery.

1915 Begins work for the Red Cross in Egypt (Alexandria), where he meets C. P. Cavafy and becomes one of the first non-Greek champions of his work.

1916 Is in danger of being called up into the army. Has his first complete sexual experience.

1919 Returns to England. Works briefly as literary editor of the *Daily Herald*. Contributes essays and reviews to a number of mostly left-wing journals.

1921 Goes to India for a second time, as private secretary to the Maharajah of Dewas State Senior. Hopes to complete *A Passage to India*, begun in 1912–13. Sees Masood again but the intensity of his love for him has passed.

1922 *Alexandria, a History and a Guide* is published. Meets J.R. Ackerley after writing him a fan-letter and arranges for him to go out to Chhatarpur.

1924 Appearance of *A Passage to India* to almost unanimous adulation. Forster inherits lease of West Hackhurst, Abinger Hammer, near Dorking, from an aunt and spends the next months arranging for the move from Weybridge.

1927 Gives the Clark Lectures at Cambridge, published the same year as *Aspects of the Novel*.

1928 He offers to appear as a witness for the defence in the trial of *The Well of Loneliness* but the judge will not allow literary evidence. *The Eternal Moment* is published.

1929 Meets a young policeman, Bob Buckingham, who becomes his closest friend for the rest of his life.

1934 Becomes president of the National Council for Civil Liberties. Collaborates with Ralph Vaughan Williams on the Abinger Pageant. Publishes *Goldsworthy Lowes Dickinson*.

1936 Publishes *Abinger Harvest* and, while still weakened by a prostate operation, has to face a possible libel action over one of the essays in it.

1938 Collaborates again with Vaughan Williams, this time on *England's Pleasant Land*, another pageant.

1940 His closest woman friend, Florence Barger, is bombed out of her London flat and goes to stay with the Forsters for eighteen months.

1941 Begins to broadcast to India for the BBC.

1942 Again serves as president of the National Council for Civil Liberties.

1944 Presides at the PEN Conference in London to celebrate the tercentenary of the publication of Milton's *Areopagitica*.

1945 Returns to India for PEN. His mother dies and he is given notice to quit West Hackhurst. Elected Honorary Fellow of King's and takes up residence in Cambridge.

1947 Pays first visit to United States to lecture at Harvard on 'The *Raison d'Etre* of Criticism in the Arts'.

1949 Returns to United States to lecture on 'Art for Art's Sake' at the Academy of Arts and Letters. Starts work on the libretto of Benjamin Britten's *Billy Budd*, in collaboration with Eric Crozier. Is offered a knighthood but declines.

1951 Publication of *Two Cheers for Democracy*.

1953 Accepts the award of Companion of Honour. *Hill of Devi* published.

1954 Florence Barger dies, after a long illness.

1956 *Marianne Thornton* is published.

1960 Appears as a witness for the defence in the *Lady Chatterley* obscenity trial.

1967 J.R. Ackerley dies.

1969 Receives the Order of Merit.

1970 7 June, dies in Coventry at the home of Bob and May Buckingham. His ashes are scattered over their rose-bed.

1971 Posthumous publication of *Maurice*.

1972 Posthumous publication of *The Life to Come*.

BIBLIOGRAPHY

The standard biography of E. M. Forster is P. N. Furbank's *E. M. Forster: A Life*, in two volumes (1977 and 1979). Both John Colmer's *E. M. Forster: The Personal Voice* (1975) and Wilfred Stone's *The Cave and the Mountain* (1965) contain biographical details, in addition to providing excellent critical insights. *Aspects of E. M. Forster* (1969), ed. Oliver Stallybrass, is largely composed of essays by friends and is an invaluable source of biographical material, particularly for the latter half of Forster's life. Of the recollections of E. M. Forster that it contains, I have been particularly indebted to 'Forster and King's' by Patrick Wilkinson and 'Forster and America' by William Roerick. In addition, I have found the following useful or worthy of note:

Ackerley, J. R. *E. M. Forster: A Portrait* (1970)

—— *The Ackerley Letters* (1975) ed. Neville Braybrooke

Annan, N. G. *Leslie Stephen: His Thought and Character in Relation to his Time* (second ed., 1984)

Bell, Quentin *Virginia Woolf: A Biography* (1972)

Beer, J. B. *The Achievement of E. M. Forster* (1962)

Bradbury, Malcolm (ed.) *Forster: A Collection Critical Essays* (1966)

Brander, L. *E. M. Forster: A Critical Study* (1968)

Connolly, Cyril *Enemies of Promise* (1938)

—— *The Condemned Playground* (1945)

Cox, C. B. *The Free Spirit: A Study of Liberal Humanism in the Novels of George Eliot, Henry James, E. M. Forster, Virginia Woolf, Angus Wilson* (1963)

Crews, F. C. *E. M. Forster: The Perils of Humanism* (1962)

De Charms, Leslie *Elizabeth of the German Garden* (1958)

Gardner, Philip (ed.) *E. M. Forster: The Critical Heritage* (1973)

Gransden, K. W. *E. M. Forster* (1962)

Hampshire, S. *Modern Writers and Other Essays* (1969)

Holroyd, Michael *Lytton Strachey: A Critical Biography* (1967, 1968)

Johnstone, J. K. *The Bloomsbury Group* (1954)

Klingopoulos, G. D. 'Mr Forster's Good Influence' in *The Modern Age* (The Pelican Guide to English Literature, vol. 7) (1961)

Lawrence, D. H. *Collected Letters* ed. Harry T. Moore (1962)

Liddell, Robert *Cavafy* (1974)

Macaulay, Rose *The Writings of E. M. Forster* (1938)

Mansfield, Katherine *The Journal of Katherine Mansfield* (1954)

McConkey, J. *The Novels of E. M. Forster* (1957)

McDowell, F. P. W. *E. M. Forster* (1969)

Pinchin, Jane L. *Alexandria Still* (1977)

Plomer, William *Autobiography* (1975)

Proctor, D. (ed) *The Autobiography of G. Lowes Dickinson* (1973)

Rowbotham S. and Weeks J. *Socialism and the New Life* (1977)

Thomson, G. H. *The Fiction of E. M. Forster* (1967)

Trilling, L. *E. M. Forster: A Study* (1944)

Woolf Leonard *Sowing: An Autobiography of the Years 1880–1904* (1960)

——*Growing: An Autobiography of the Years 1904–1911* (1961)

——*Beginning Again: 1911–1918* (1964)

——*Down Hill all the Way: 1919–1939* (1967) (Now available in 2 vols., reissued in 1980.)

Woolf, Virginia *The Letters, Vols 1–6* (1975–80) ed. Nigel Nicholson and J. Trautmann.

——*The Diary, Vols 1–5* (1977–84) ed. Anne Olivier Bell.

E. M. FORSTER'S WRITINGS

NOVELS AND SHORT STORIES
Where Angels Fear to Tread (1905); *The Longest Journey* (1907); *A Room with a View* (1908); *Howards End* (1910); *The Celestial Omnibus* (1911); *A Passage to India* (1924); *The Eternal Moment* (1928); *Maurice* (1971); *The Life to Come* (1972).

BIOGRAPHY
Goldsworthy Lowes Dickinson (1934); *Marianne Thornton* (1956).

LETTERS
Selected Letters of E. M. Forster ed. P. N. Furbank and Mary Lago. (Two volumes, 1983 and 1985.)

OTHER:
Alexandria: A History and a Guide (1922); *Pharos and Pharillon* (1923); *Aspects of the Novel* (1927); *Abinger Harvest* (1936); *Two Cheers for Democracy* (1951); *The Hill of Devi* (1953).

The Abinger Edition (ed. Oliver Stallybrass) is the standard scholarly edition of Forster's writings. It includes the hitherto unpublished novel *Arctic Summer* — which Forster never finished — and material which has previously appeared only in newspapers and periodicals. A facsimile edition of Forster's *Commonplace Book* was published in 1978 by Scolar Press.

Forster's novels, stories and essays are all published in paperback in the UK and US in various editions.

Acknowledgments

In addition to the published sources cited above, I should like to express my gratitude for information provided by: the late Mr J. R. Ackerley; Mrs Molly Barger; Mrs Marion Boyars; Mr Neville Braybrooke; Mrs May Buckingham; Mrs Sylvia Buckingham; Mr Sandy Campbell; the late Sir Malcolm Darling; Mr John Morris; and Mr Brian Taylor. I am deeply indebted to the late Oliver Stallybrass for his suggestions and criticisms on reading this book in draft.

LIST OF ILLUSTRATIONS

60 Forrest Reid; painting by James Sleator, 1924. *Collection Ulster Museum, Belfast*

61 E.M. Forster, 1923; drawing by Sir William Rothenstein. *Photo courtesy Sotheby Parke Bernet and Co.*

62 The Pharos at Alexandria, reverse of coin of Antoninus Pius (AD 138–61). *British Museum*

63 Montazah Palace, Alexandria, Red Cross Hospital in World War I. *Photo courtesy Egyptian Tourist Office*

64 E.M. Forster in Alexandria. *By permission of the Provost and Scholars of King's College, Cambridge*

65 Mohammed-el-Adl. *By permission of the Provost and Scholars of King's College, Cambridge*

66 C.P. Cavafy. *By permission of George Savidis*

67 The salon of C.P. Cavafy. *By permission of George Savidis*

70 E.M. Forster in India, 1921. *By permission of the Provost and Scholars of King's College, Cambridge*

71 Group including in front row the Maharajah of Dewas State Senior, his son and Mr and Mrs Agg. *By permission of the Provost and Scholars of King's College, Cambridge*

72 The Hill of Devi, Dewas State, India. *By permission of the Provost and Scholars of King's College, Cambridge*

73 Virginia Woolf, 1912; portrait by Vanessa Bell. *Private collection. Photo Courtauld Institute of Art*

73 Leonard Woolf and Goldsworthy Lowes Dickinson at Asheham House, 1914. *By permission of Mrs M.T. Parsons and Hogarth Press*

75 Tennis party in India, c. 1910. *Radio Times Hulton Picture Library*

76 Charles Mauron at Saint-Rémy-de Provence, 1938. *Photo J. de Beucken*

77 W.H. Auden, Christopher Isherwood and Stephen Spender, c. 1936; photo by Howard Coster. *National Portrait Gallery*

78 J.R. Ackerley and his sister Nancy. *Courtesy Richard Shone*

78 E.M. Forster at Monk's House, Rodmell; photo by Leonard Woolf. *By permission of Professor Quentin Bell*

78 E.M. Forster with J.R. Ackerley by Chiswick Reach. *Private collection*

79 E.M. Forster at St Mawes, Cornwall.

80 E.M. Forster, 1930; drawing by Edmond Kapp. *By permission of the Provost and Scholars of King's College, Cambridge*

81 H.O. Meredith, 1938. *Photo Ramsey and Muspratt, Cambridge*

82 Robert Buckingham. *By permission of the Provost and Scholars of King's College, Cambridge*

83 E.M. Forster and Robert Buckingham. *By permission of the Provost and Scholars of King's College, Cambridge*

83 E.M. Forster and Robert Buckingham. *Photo Spender*

Edmiston. *Courtesy Mrs M. Buckingham*

84 West Hackhurst, Abinger, Surrey. *By permission of the Provost and Scholars of King's College, Cambridge*

85 Entrance to 1–10 Arlington Park Mansions, Chiswick. *Greater London County Photo Library*

87 T.E. Lawrence as aircraftman Shaw, 1935; drawing by Augustus John. *Ashmolean Museum, Oxford*

89 Una Lady Troubridge and Miss Radclyffe Hall with their dachshunds, at the 1923 Cruft's Dog Show. *Radio Times Hulton Picture Library*

90 The Memoir Club, 1943 (*on the left* Duncan Grant, Vanessa Bell, David Garnett, *second row* Leonard Woolf, Clive Bell, J.M. Keynes and Lydia Lopokova-Keynes, *on the right* E.M. Forster, Quentin Bell, Molly and Desmond MacCarthy); painting by Vanessa Bell. *By permission of Professor Quentin Bell*

91 E.M. Forster, 1940; caricature by Max Beerbohm. *By permission of the Provost and Scholars of King's College, Cambridge*

91 E.M. Forster; portrait by Vanessa Bell, c. 1940. *Private collection. Photo Courtauld Institute of Art*

92 E.M. Forster at Lytton Strachey's house Ham Spray.

94 Lady Allen of Hurtwood, E.M. Forster, and Ralph Vaughan Williams discussing the Abinger Pageant, 1934. *By permission of Miss Polly Allen*

95 Map of Abinger, 1937. *By permission of the Provost and Scholars of King's College, Cambridge*

96 Mrs Florence Barger. *Courtesy Estate of Mrs F. Barger*

97 E. M. Forster with Frank Franklyn, Rooksnest Farm, 1949. *By permission of the Provost and Scholars of King's College, Cambridge*

98 E. M. Forster in India, 1945. *By permission of the Provost and Scholars of King's College, Cambridge*

99 Rabindranath Tagore. *Courtesy of College of Tagore Studies, Santiniketan, India*

100 E. M. Forster and his mother at West Hackhurst, Abinger, Surrey. *By permission of the Provost and Scholars of King's College, Cambridge*

100 G. H. W. Rylands, 1973. *Photo Philip Gaskell*

101 E. M. Forster in his rooms at King's College. *Courtesy John Morris*

102 E. M. Forster at Stoneblossom, New Jersey, June 1949. *Photo Glenway Westcott*

103 E. M. Forster working on the libretto of Benjamin Britten's opera *Billy Budd*, with Britten in

background. *Radio Times Hulton Picture Library*

103 Theodor Uppman in the role of Billy Budd, at the Royal Opera House, 1951. *Photo Roger Wood*

104 J. R. Ackerley, photographed by Francis King at Nara, Japan, 1960.

105 E. M. Forster after the performance of *Howards End* at the Golder's Green Hippodrome (*from left to right* Gwen Wetford, Michael Goodliffe, Andrew Ray and Vanessa Forsyth), February 1967. *Press Association*

106 Order of Merit (*top*) and Companion of Honour medals. *Courtesy Messrs Spink and Son, London*

107 E. M. Forster in the foothills of the Alps. *By permission of the Provost and Scholars of King's College, Cambridge*

108 E. M. Forster and Donald Windham in the grounds of King's College, 1960. *Photo Sandy Cambell*

109 E. M. Forster and Christopher Isherwood, at King's College, 14 March 1970. *Photo Mark Lancaster*

109 E. M. Forster with Tom Coley at King's College, January 1969. *Photo W. Roerick*

109 E. M. Forster with William Roerick, King's College, January 1969. *Photo Tom Coley*

110 May Buckingham, John Morris, William Plomer and E. M. Forster. *Courtesy John Morris*

111 May Buckingham and E. M. Forster, at Aldeburgh, Suffolk. *Courtesy Mrs M. Buckingham*

111 E. M. Forster and Robert Buckingham, Fawsley Park, 1968. *Courtesy Mrs M. Buckingham*

112 E. M. Forster and Sir John Wolfenden during a broadcast in the BBC General Overseas Service, 1958. *Photo copyright BBC*

113 E. M. Forster with cat. *Courtesy Mrs S. Buckingham*

114 Detail from *What I believe*; painting by Paul Cadmus, 1948. *By permission of the Provost and Scholars of King's College, Cambridge*

115 E. M. Forster, about to appear as witness at trial of *Lady Chatterley's Lover*, 28 October 1960. *The Associated Press*

117 E. M. Forster in his bedroom at King's College, Cambridge. *Photo Cecil Beaton/Camera Press*

INDEX